Stubborn Faith

Foreword by **Rev. Bimbo Arowojolu**

Stubborn Faith

LAWRENCE OJI

Dedicated to **Rev. Dr. Femi Idowu**

ISBN: 9798876757296

Bible versions used include:

DEDICATION

I am most delighted to dedicate this book on Faith to you my beloved brother, Dr. Femi Bosun Idowu (FBI — "Dominion Ground" as I fondly called you). You were a Christian par excellence, an erudite teacher of the Word who lived by what he preached and believed in, an exemplary Pastor and a renowned medical practitioner.

Firstly, I thank God Almighty who made our paths cross, and I also thank Rev. Tayo Arowojolu who insisted I got close to you in the church when you were with us as his associate Pastor all the way back at 800a High Road, Tottenham.

To borrow one of the words you never missed using, I never realised that the hard man I thought you were was just a 'façade' or something that existed only in my imagination. When I got closer to you, I found out that you were one of the finest gentlemen alive with a heart of pure gold and a fear of God. I discovered that you were a good man whose motto was to do good at all times to as many people as God brought your way.

You were one medical doctor who took delight in praying for your patients and committing their issues to the Doctor of all doctors, Jesus Christ whom you loved without apologies. You believed totally in the words of Jesus Christ in **Matthew 19:26**, that what was impossible to doctors was possible with Doctor Jesus. You prayed for patients who wanted you to do so and never tried to offend people of other faiths by praying for them openly, yet you never ceased to make intercessions for them at their backs. How can I forget how God used you to save the life of our first daughter, Favour? Your wise counsel and unflinching faith helped us take the firm decision not to cave in when one of the Consultant Doctors insisted on a treatment that would have led to my wife losing that pregnancy. Your wise counsel still echoes in my ears. You said, "Bro Solution, we have prayed, I would say let's stand by the prayers", and that is exactly what we did! And the Lord showed up. Today, my daughter is 14. Thank you, my beloved brother.

To demonstrate your trust in God and in His infallible Word, you put it down in your book, *God's Pill,* prescribing one capsule per day at the least, recommending that there is no risk of overdose. Your son, Olaofe in his tribute at the Service of Songs summed it all up in one word, "Intentional". Yes, that is what you were.

You were passionate about raising "Thinking Christians" and the result is evident. You pastored New Covenant Church, Strong Nation for only three years and you left an indelible footprint on the sands of time there my brother. You taught and practised "giving" but also taught them never to "give-in".

You were truly a man of faith whose favourite scriptures were particularly Psalm 1 "*Blessed is the man who doesn't stand, walk or sit with the scornful*", and **Romans 3:3-4 [NKJV]** which says,

> "*For what if some did not believe? Will their unbelief make the faithfulness of God without effect? Certainly not! Indeed, let God be true but every man a liar. As it is written: "That You may be justified in Your words and may overcome when You are judged."*

I still remember the last time you appeared to me in my dream, and I asked you how it is over where you are. In response, you fell on the ground and raised your two legs up in the air like a little child, giggling and said to me, "Brother Solution, Jesus is so humorous! He keeps you on your toes laughing all day long."

Thank you for the privilege you gave me of seeing you EVERY DAY and sharing your last 40 days on earth with you. Initially, we would pray DAILY until you decided we should stop praying for healing and should instead start Praising Him only, which we did until the end. I know you saw heaven opened even before you went there, and it was evident that you were happy to go and be with this Jesus you so loved finally, having completed your mission and ministry here.

Like Paul said in the Book of Philippians, you remaining here would have been for us, because as far as you were concerned, to live is Christ and to die is gain.

Heaven rejoices for having a jewel back home. I echo your son, OlaOfe, you were indeed INTENTIONAL!

Once more, man of demonstrable faith, Rev Femi Idowu, this book is dedicated to you.

ENDORSEMENT

REV. WILLIAMS A. OLANIYI

I count it such a great privilege and honour for me to endorse this crucial exploration of the subject of FAITH, penned by a great servant of God in the Body of Christ, Evangelist Lawrence Oji. His genuine encounter with God that brought him salvation, as beautifully documented in his book, *From Prison to Pulpit*, marks the beginning of his faith journey.

The author's daily lifestyle of looking up to God as his Source, Strength and Sustainer is further proof of his faith in God. Writing on the great subject of faith without a genuine encounter with God is like a blind person in a typical village describing the beauty of colours to those with two functional eyes. If there is someone qualified by the grace of God to write on the great subject of Faith, the author is one.

It is crucial to emphasise that genuine knowledge of God is paramount for the practice of faith; it cannot be achieved solely by enhancing our learning, attitude, or behaviour. Our starting point is to die to the flesh and be BORN AGAIN to initiate fellowship with God (1 John 1:1-3). After all, God's kind of faith is acquired and practised through His holy words (Romans 10:17).

FAITH is a major subject in the school of working and walking with God on His terms and conditions. It is such an important subject that, without it, we CANNOT please God (Hebrews 11:6).

In this great piece, *Stubborn Faith*, the author was able to do justice to what faith is not, what faith is, the source of faith, and levels of faith, among others—all with biblical quotations and sandwiched powerfully with his personal examples of faith demonstration to help you know more of the truth about faith.

Stubborn Faith can be defined as acting on the word of God with resolute determination not to change one's stance or position until the manifestation of God's act. Hear the author's words whilst operating faith for a dead man to come alive again:

> *"Rather than worry about what I was seeing (a dead man on the floor), I chose to hold onto the word I had received earlier on at Qatar airport, "Stubborn Faith.""*

Nothing operates in the kingdom of God outside faith, the principal instrument for obtaining heaven-approved results on earth. Everything works by faith in God.

In one of my books titled *The Faith that Conquers*, I talked about the simple process of faith operation by making use of the acronym F-A-I-T-H. This will surely help you to practise *Stubborn Faith* with undeniable results, as documented in this book by the author, Evangelist Lawrence Oji. Here is the acronym:

F- Find the relevant word of God to stand on for your situation.
A- Act on the word of God.
I- Insist on obeying the word of God.
T- Talk to God continually in prayers.
H- Hold on till the end.

Through my relationship with the person, shared experiences/encounters, family interactions, and the writing and preaching ministry of the author, I recommend this well-loaded book to anyone who desires to know more about faith in God. *Stubborn Faith* in God is able to enable those who are unable to be able. Prepare for an unforgettable encounter as you read through this book with an open mind.

Williams A. Olaniyi
Mount Zion Global Ministries &
Hope House International UK.
Author of Locating the helpers of destiny.

CONTENTS

ACKNOWLEDGEMENT

Let me start by thanking God Almighty for the privilege to be alive and to be saved. Even though the grace that brings salvation has appeared to all men and God wants all men to be saved, Jesus said in **John 6:44,** *"No man can come to Me unless My Father draws him."* I thank God for drawing me to Jesus Christ.

I want to thank my Pastor, Tayo Arowojolu for all the support given to me right from the day our paths crossed over 20 years ago. Thank you, Pastor Bimbo Arowojolu (fondly called Sis Bimbo) for writing the Foreword of this book, STUBBORN FAITH", a topic I am sure you must have found easy to deal with, seeing how stubborn your faith was when you were confronted with a very serious situation not quite long ago. The calm you displayed was unbelievable. You did not let anyone into what you were facing, but chose to trust this God without betraying any anxiety. I admire your faith.

I thank you very much my brother and my friend Pastor Damian Luke. The advice and the encouragement you gave me to go for Masters in Theology will always be remembered. God bless you. I thank my friend and my brother from another mother, Rev. Williams

Olaniyi for all the guidance and suggestions you always provided whenever I call you. God did not preserve your life from the knives of those killers for no reason. You are making sure you impact people's lives daily. May God bless you. My appreciation also goes to my brother, Dr. Innocent Izamoje for painstakingly reading through the manuscript in one night and making invaluable suggestions. Sir, you are a good man. Your humility is out of this world.

I want to appreciate you seriously, Rev. Enny Idowu, (Dottoressa Eleganza as I fondly call you), for being such a wonderful woman with a heart of gold. Your labour of love shall not be forgotten by God. That statement you made on that fateful day, "I'm now married to Jesus"; He heard it and I pray He will use you beyond your wildest imaginations and make you the Kathleen Kuhlman of these last days in terms of miraculous works. I thank you Pastor Sade Arise, (Arise and Shine) for your wonderful support. Your kindness will constantly speak as a memorial for you before God. Thank you, sister Folake Kuti. Your love and your humility will make a way for you. Sister Elizabeth Falana, may the Lord reward your kindness. I sincerely appreciate all the Coordinators of Living Waters Ministry. You are indeed a family. Thank you for "adopting" me as one of you.

My special thanks also go to Rev Dr. Olaniran and his wife and BEST friend in NCC, Rome, Italy. May the Lord add to your shopping basket what you did not order. You both are the true definition of Christianity. You are so unassuming. May the Lord remember you for good. I love you sir and ma.

I thank you Pastor Jimi Akinola. You are always operating from behind closed doors, yet the impact you make without making any noise is worthy of emulation. You are a gentleman to the core. May the Lord reward you unbelievably.

Brother Patrick and sister Pat Enenmoh, when our paths crossed, I realised that indeed as the saying goes in my place, "nwanne di n amba" truly. You have demonstrated to be the brother and sister the Lord prepared for me in a foreign/distant land. I admire you loads.

I appreciate you loads my dear brother, Dr. Uche Orji for your kindness towards the family. You are a man of integrity. My country Nigeria needs more public servants like yourself. You have proven that it is possible to serve in a public office and leave a great legacy without being corrupt. I am very proud to say you are my brother. I am very proud of you. Be ready to receive a great reward from above. You haven't seen anything yet. God bless you.

I thank all the members of our Evangelism Team and the NCC Edmonton family for the love you show me as my family.

I thank my girls, my anointed Princesses, Favour and Esther for all your support and the peace I enjoy being your daddy. You both make being a daddy easy for me, seeing I had no prior experience before God gave you to me. I am so proud to be called your father.

Finally, my hugs, my embrace, my kisses are reserved for you, my POTATOMATO, UGOZAMBA STAINLESS STAR STELLA-MARIS EKPENE OJI, my wife of inestimable value, my HIBISCUS, my Angel. You are indeed a rare gem. Many men go out looking for a wife but in my own case, God gave you to me **(Proverbs 19:14).** Without you in my life I would never have written one book, (even though I have books inside of me as a result of the experiences I have had in my lifetime so far), but your support and your push spurred me on to become an author of so many books. You are a VERY good woman. May the Lord keep us both alive in good health so that you will reap this love you have deposited in the bank of my heart. I love you, my STAR.

Pastor Lawrence "Solution" Oji
MA THEOLOGY (Roehampton University London)

FOREWORD

REV. BIMBO AROWOJOLU

Who else would be better positioned to write a book on Faith, if not Pastor Lawrence Oji (aka Solution)? This is a man who has seen it all: from a life of drug addiction with its attendant prison cycles spanning nearly three decades to complete restoration by Christ Jesus; saved purely by GRACE and now witnessing for Christ. Only a man with such a past will understand what it is to 'live by faith'. Yes, he is well qualified to write about 'Stubborn or Radical faith'.

Faith is without question one of the most important fundamental subjects that underlines the Christian belief and perhaps one of the most misconstrued. But Pastor Solution has broken down this seemingly complex subject into small bites easy for the reader to grasp and digest; he has presented the message in its simplest and practical form without losing the potency. Such articulation can only come from a man whose faith is enmeshed in God.

Brother Solution as I call him, writes from the heart. He need not conduct any research on Faith as his life experiences alone would suffice. He talks about Faith that does not consult the senses for realities; faith that is rooted in a conviction that God's Word is final. He calls it 'the God kind of Faith'. He writes that each of us has been given "a measure of this faith" as recorded in **Romans 12:3.** This means that we all start out with the same measure. Every person who accepts Christ as his or her personal Saviour has faith!

This is the general theme that is woven throughout every chapter of the book. Lawrence lays emphasis on the fact that this kind of faith is already in us; we were born again with it in our spirits. All we need to do is to stir it up! Let it saturate our whole being. He urges us to have an attitude of one that has already overcome; no matter the challenges that may come our way. He insists that we need strong, stubborn faith that persistently holds on to God, holds Him to His promises, and will not let go. He pleads that we walk in this consciousness confident that come what may, the Lord will always come through for us **(Romans 8:31).**

Using humour, illustrations, and relevant scriptures, Lawrence shares many practical demonstrations of faith; the trials, tragedies and ultimate victories from his own family and ministry. His writing style is impressive and makes for an interesting read! The message is apt especially in today's era of 'Microwave' Christianity where everything is about 'now'.

I have known Pastor Solution for over twenty years, he is a man who 'walks the talk', a man with an unrivalled passion for soul winning and a genuine desire to see every believer access the promises of God by faith. I found "Stubborn Faith" engaging and insightful and far from an academic exercise. There is no doubt that this book will become the 'go to' manual for every Christian who desires to live a victorious life in Christ. I strongly recommend it to every believer (and people of other faith), I urge you to read every testimony recorded in this book as it will help build your faith for when you are faced with that challenging situation. Surely, challenging times will come.

Rev. Bimbo Arowojolu
Co-Lead Pastor,
New Covenant Church, Edmonton

PREFACE

The date was the 24th of October 2017 and I was on my way to Lahore in the Islamic Republic of Pakistan. A branch of our church (New Covenant Church) had invited me for a three weeks' programme. As the plane taxied in readiness for take-off, I found myself uttering a word of prayer and asking the Lord what message He would have me kickstart the programme with.

Very soon, we were airborne, and I still hadn't received a response until we had a three hour stop over at Qatar airport. It was then that the Lord whispered in my spirit, "STUBBORN FAITH". I was a bit taken aback because out of all the messages I prepared, none was about faith. To make matters worse, the programme was to start that same evening as soon as I arrived.

Not wanting to disobey the Holy Spirit, I knew that I was not going to start with any other message except that one He spoke into my ears in answer to my question. Initially, a sense of panic gripped me as I knew I did not have sufficient time to prepare that message and starting with one of the many messages I had prepared for the duration of my stay in Lahore was not an option.

But I was also fascinated by the topic 'Stubborn Faith'. I had preached many messages on faith in the past, but none was titled 'Stubborn Faith'. I began to ponder on the term all through the journey and at the same time thinking how to prepare the sermon.

The moment I boarded the connecting flight from Qatar to Lahore, I asked the Holy Spirit to help me download what exactly He would want me to preach on that topic. I cannot remember now how long the journey was but before I arrived at Lahore airport, the Lord had helped me write down a few things about Stubborn faith, without obviously letting me into what was ahead. All I can say here is that it is in our own interest to obey the Holy Spirit even if we either think what He wants us to do doesn't make any sense to us, or we think we know some other thing we can do which may seem "better" in our own understanding. How on earth would I have known that the Lord was going to glorify Himself in a manner I would never have imagined, by raising a dead man on that day and straightening a foot that had been bent from birth? Our God indeed works in mysterious ways.

It was indeed a demonstration of Stubborn Faith. It pays indeed to obey God's voice and the nudging or the prompting of the Holy Spirit.

In fact, after what happened during the Pakistani trip, I now understand better what the word of God says in **Proverbs 3:5-6 (AMP):**

"Lean on, trust in, and be confident in the Lord with all your heart and mind and do not rely on your own insight or understanding. In all your ways know, recognize, and acknowledge Him, and He will direct and make straight and plain your paths."

INTRODUCTION

'Stubborn Faith' as given to me by the inspiration of the Holy Spirit borders on the need to exercise our faith in God and watch the Lord come through for us especially in those seemingly impossible situations.

I felt the need to write this book based on the encounter I had with the Lord Jesus on my trip to Lahore in the Islamic Republic of Pakistan. This single encounter has changed my whole outlook on life; it has reinforced my belief in the subject of faith, increased my resolve to depend on God completely and to trust Him like a child.

I can tell you that walking by faith is not always the easiest of things to do. When life is hard and suffering is heavy, it can be extremely difficult to live by faith but the righteous and just are to walk by faith and trust that all will be well in the Lord.

Today's world is an incredibly distracting, busy, tempting and chaotic place, full of responsibilities, duties, hobbies and pleasures. You can believe in Christianity as firmly as you believe you know your own given name, but belief does not always translate to practising and living creeds in daily life. It's not always that easy to follow the biblical prescription of walking by faith and not by sight.

Walking by faith can seem mysterious. After all, there is no faith thermometer to indicate how hot or cold your faith walk is. There is also no fuel gauge to measure how full or empty your faith level is. And before you think that faith is only a religious thing that some people have as a life-supplement to help get through the tough times, remember this:

Everyone lives by faith. Yes, it might sound shocking, but we all live by faith according to Kenneth Hagin who is considered the pioneer of the faith movement.

Perhaps you are asking how? This is evident by the simple things that we do daily. For instance, when you drive down the motorway, you are living by faith that others will obey the traffic laws. When you get on any flight, you are living by faith that the pilot that you don't see will get you safely to your destination. When you fill-up your car at the petrol station, you are living by faith that the amount of fuel pumping into your car (which you can't see) matches the exact number of gallons you are being charged (which you can see). The truth though is that some attendants in some countries know how to manipulate and tamper with the pumps such that the fuel that goes into the tank doesn't equate to the fuel that you are being charged, yet you pay because you believe the obvious.

It is equally true that we make hundreds of faith decisions daily. We all live by faith! Simply put, faith is the confidence you have in something or someone.

The real question is, where do we put our faith? As Christians, we are to put our faith in God. We are to trust Him completely. Blind Trust is the absolute requirement. No wonder Jesus says in the Book of **Matthew 18:3,**

> *"Assuredly, I say to you, unless you are converted and become as little children, you will by no means enter the kingdom of heaven."*

This is because little children don't have time to doubt. They believe blindly. Their faith in their parents is total, complete and unshakeable.

The main purpose of writing this book, therefore, is so that anyone who is still struggling with trusting God by believing in Him and standing on His infallible promises can learn from my own experiences. I am trusting the Lord that by the time you've read this book halfway, your own faith in God will have become so stubborn and radical that you would not get to the end of the book before you start telling other people that faith in the Lord is the ONLY currency one needs in order to appropriate all of God's promises.

I have tasted God's faithfulness in my own life! How do you explain that a chronic prisoner, a drug addict of several years, who had given up even on himself and on life, is now witnessing Christ and hope to others? This transformation has been simply through my BLIND FAITH in God.

I can only agree with the Word of God in the Book of **Jeremiah 17:7-8 (AMP),**

> *"[Most] blessed is the man who believes in, trusts in, and relies on the Lord, and whose hope and confidence the Lord is. For he shall be like a tree by the waters that spreads out its roots by the river; and it shall not see and fear when heat comes; but its leaf shall be green. It shall not be anxious and full of care in the year of drought, nor shall it cease yielding fruit."*

My advocation is for you to read the book with an open mind, release your faith and trust the Lord to come through for that situation. My intention is not to treat Faith as an academic subject! My write-up is based on personal experiences that I believe will help grow that 'Measure of Faith' that has been given to all of us as Christians.

CHAPTER 1
HEAVEN'S CURRENCY

*"What we have seen and [ourselves] heard,
we are also telling you, so that you too may realise and enjoy fellowship
as partners and partakers with us. And [this] fellowship that we have
[which is a distinguishing mark of Christians] is with the Father and
with His Son Jesus Christ (the Messiah)."*
1 John 1:3 [AMP]

The subject of faith is perhaps one of the most talked about and one of the most referenced in Christendom. It is a central theme in the kingdom of God. In many instances, it's been referred to as the currency that Heaven uses.

In simple terms, currency is the money that a country uses. In the UK, it's the pound sterling. Different countries have different currencies. Imagine you want to purchase items worth two hundred pounds (£200); you go to the storekeeper with the monetary value of that item and he or she hands you the item. Your transaction is done. The same way you make these purchases with currencies is the same way that Faith is the 'currency' by which you make transactions in the Kingdom. In the natural realm, we exchange money for the things we want and need. But in the spiritual realm, faith is what we exchange. The Bible tells us that when we pray, if we have faith, we will receive what we pray for. The currency spent and accepted in one country may not be accepted in another country where they spend a different currency. Heaven has its own acceptable currency and that currency is called FAITH.

Faith is therefore, heaven's currency. The Bible records in **Romans 4:9** that Faith was CREDITED to Abraham as Righteousness... this goes to show that Abraham PURCHASED Righteousness with the currency called Faith. NOTHING can be gotten from the Kingdom without faith. It is undisputedly the currency that we need.

Faith moves mountains. Faith opens supernatural doors. Faith pleases God. Faith is the main anchor on which our confession as Christians rest. The Bible records that without Faith, it is impossible to please God. And I dare say that without Faith, it is impossible to even know God in the right way. When you do not have faith, you will find it difficult to satisfy God's principles that guide the life of mankind. Not just the faith to receive something from God, but even the faith to trust in the love of God that although things are not in the way they thought they should be, God is still able to make things right. If you do not know the subject of faith, you will not know how to increase it and grow into the stature of Christ.

In fact, ANYTHING done outside of faith is a sin **[Romans 14:23]**! This implies that so long as the Kingdom is concerned, Faith is the only means by which you can make any transaction. Even the SALVA-TION of your soul was received by FAITH **[Ephesians 2:8]**.

God Himself demonstrated His faith when He created the Heavens and the Earth. In Genesis Chapter 1, God said, "Let there be Light", and there was light. God spoke things that BE NOT as though they were **[Romans 4:17]**. He said, *"Light be! And light was"!*

Our fellowship with God and His Son Jesus Christ is through our FAITH in the grace that brings salvation. There is no limit to where you can get to provided you place a demand on God's promises by FAITH. **Ephesians 2:8-9** [NIV] reads,

> *"For it is by grace you have been saved, through FAITH and this is not from yourselves, it is the gift of God, not by works, so that no one can boast'."*

It must be worth pointing out that Grace will not work until you place a demand. For emphasis, there is absolutely no limit for the anointing provided you place a demand through the exercise of your FAITH in the matchless and most powerful name of Jesus Christ. Even though **Titus 2:11** says that the grace of God that brings salvation has appeared to all men, we still cannot appropriate that salvation except through FAITH in our Lord and Saviour, Jesus Christ. **John 1:12** says that as many as received Him, He gave them power to become the sons of God. After Peter spoke to the lame man in front of the Beautiful Gate and he walked, to explain what transpired to those who were perplexed at the miracle, Peter said to them in **Acts 3:16** [AMP],

> *"And His name, through and by FAITH in His name, has made this man whom you see and recognise well and strong. [Yes] the FAITH which is through and by Him [Jesus] has given the man this perfect soundness [of body] before all of you."*

I therefore invite you to enjoy fellowship with the Lord by releasing your faith to walk with God.

THIS THING CALLED FAITH: WHAT IS IT?

Before I try to explain what FAITH is, I would like to explain what FAITH is not.

FAITH is neither assumption nor presumption. Let us look at the word assume for a moment. According to the Oxford Dictionary, the definition is; "to pretend to have or be, to take as granted or true, suppose to be the case, without proof."

Let us also look at "presumption," a synonym for assume.

> "It is an idea that is taken to be true and often used as the basis for other ideas, although it is not known for certain."

To assume you know what God will do is to be presumptuous, which is to be in a dangerous position.

FAITH must be based on and backed by God's Word. Whatever assignment God gives He backs up. If He gives the vision, He will also make a provision so the vision will be realised. He is FAITHFUL to His Word. The Bible says that God cannot lie. [Titus 1:2]. There are two things God cannot do. God cannot lie and He cannot die. **Deuteronomy 32:40** says that God cannot die. He lives forever. **Numbers 23:19** says that God is not a man that He should lie. Has He said it and shall He not bring it to pass? If He says it, He will defend it. If He didn't say it and you are presumptuous, you may have the greatest regrets of your life. As a matter of fact, it is written in the Book of **Jeremiah 23:31** [AMP],

> "Behold, I am against the prophets, says the Lord, who use their [own deceitful] tongues and say, thus says the Lord."

If He says it, He will back you up and you will not fall on the way.

David was a king and God sent a mere man, Gad, to go to him and deliver a message that was intended as a reproach to the king. He went to the king and delivered the message and David couldn't harm or hurt him. [1 Chronicles 21]. God always backs His Word. All He wants from us is to exercise our FAITH. Also In **1 Kings 13:1-4**, God sent a young Prophet to go and prophecy the destruction of the altar king Jeroboam used for sacrifices, and Jeroboam couldn't hurt him because he had God's backing. As a matter of fact, his hand dried up when he pointed it towards God's Messenger commanding that he should be arrested.

On the contrary, if God didn't say it and we just walk by assumption, we will suffer the consequences. There are many people doing many things under the guise of Faith, when in fact, it is not Faith at all: it is Foolishness, and in most cases, it is Presumption. For example, a few years ago in Nigeria, one Pastor Daniel, in an attempt to prove the faithfulness of God, went to a zoo and jumped into a lion's cage simply because he read how God shut the lion's mouth in the Book of Daniel 6. Within a few minutes, in the full glare of people, the lions tore him apart. That was foolishness. Jesus said in **Matthew 4:7**, *"You shall not tempt the Lord your God."*

We must know how to differentiate FAITH from assumption or presumption.

What then is Faith, you may ask. FAITH is saying to God, "No matter what it costs me, I'm going to trust You and whatever You say."

In **John 6:67-69** [MSG], after some disciples left Jesus, the bible records the following:

> *"Then Jesus gave the twelve their chance: "Do you also want to leave?" Peter replied. "Master, to whom would we go? You have the words of REAL life, eternal life. We've already committed ourselves, confident that You are the Holy One of God."*

FAITH is hanging in there even when everything else doesn't make any sense, simply because you know Whom you have believed. This is evident in **2 Timothy 1:12 [NLT]**. It says,

> *"That is why I am suffering here in prison. But I am not ashamed of it, for I know the One in whom I trust, and I am sure that He is able to guard what I have entrusted to Him until the day of His return."*

Faith is to believe what you do not see and you are rewarded with seeing what you believed. It is believing God and believing His Word because God and His Word are one and the same. In the beginning was the Word, the Word was with God, and the Word was God **[John 1:1]**. That Word became flesh (Jesus) in **John 1:14** and dwelt among us. Revelations 19:13 also supports that the name of Jesus Christ is the Word of God. It makes no sense to have faith in God and not have the same faith in His word. Faith is not optimism or an intellectual decision. Faith is a gift from God to us. We don't produce it on our own; it is our response for trusting God.

Someone once said that "In the world seeing is believing, whereas in the Word, believing is seeing." In **John 11:40**, Jesus was at the tomb of Lazarus who had been dead for four days and He commanded that the stone that was used to cover the tomb be removed. Martha, Lazarus's sister's concern was that four days had passed and that it would be of no use to remove the stone. Jesus said to her,

> *"Did I not say to you that if you would BELIEVE you would SEE the glory of God?"*

FAITH DEFINED

There are various definitions of faith but for the purpose of this book and what I am aiming to achieve, I will focus on two definitions of faith, namely: the Dictionary definition of faith and the Biblical definition.

The English Dictionary Definition of FAITH (Merriam-Webster)

Faith is a strong belief or trust in someone or somebody; belief in the existence of God; strong religious beliefs. The emphasis really is primarily about a firm belief in something for which there is no proof; a complete trust.

The Cambridge Dictionary Definition

The belief that someone or something is good, right, and able to be trusted.

Formal Definition of Faith

Faith, derived from Latin *fides* and Old French *feid*, is confidence or trust in a person, thing, or concept. In the context of religion, faith is "belief in God or in the doctrine or teachings of religion."

The Bible Definition of FAITH

The ultimate definition of faith in the Bible is found in the Book of **Hebrews 11:1** which without doubt will be quoted repeatedly in various places throughout this book, albeit from different translations.

- **Hebrews 11:1 [NKJV]** – *Now FAITH is the substance of things hoped for, the evidence of things not seen.*
- **Hebrews 11:1 [AMP]** – *Now FAITH is the assurance (the confirmation, the title deed) of the things [we] hope for, being the proof of things [we] do not see and the conviction of their*

reality [faith perceiving as real fact what is not revealed to the senses].

- **Hebrews 11:1 [NLT]** – *FAITH is the confident assurance that what we hope for is going to happen. It is the evidence of things we cannot yet see.*
- **Hebrews 11:1 [MSG]** – *The fundamental fact of existence is that this trust in God, this FAITH, is the firm foundation under everything that makes life worth living. It is our handle on what we can't see.*
- **Hebrews 11:1 [TPT]** – *Now faith brings our hopes into reality and becomes the foundation needed to acquire the things we long for. It is all the evidence required to prove what is still unseen.*

Hopefully these different translations give you a better idea of what faith is!

Kenneth Hagin in one of his books defines faith as 'the hand that takes the things of God'. I pondered on this definition, and it makes total sense. Faith is the hand that takes the invisible things of God and brings them into manifestation in the physical realm. It is like the eye that sees beyond the natural and receives things from the supernatural. Faith is taking a promise of God and confessing it with full confidence till it becomes a reality in your life. Faith is receiving a promise of God without seeing any visible evidence of it. Faith is receiving the things of God solely upon what His Word says! It is not based on physical evidence because if you could physically see it, then the entire need for faith would become obsolete and unnecessary. Faith is believing the Word of God regardless of your situation, circumstances, and problem.

In the words of Dave Wills, "FAITH is a choice to trust God even when the road ahead seems uncertain." FAITH is not something to apply in the future but in the present.

As a matter of fact, the definition of FAITH in the Bible starts with the word, "NOW" as seen in **Hebrews 11:1**. It didn't say THEN, faith was... NOR did it say, LATER, faith WILL BE... it says NOW FAITH IS... this goes to show that faith is in the present!

The demonstration of FAITH is this: You don't know what's next but you trust God to show up and take care of you. That same scripture says faith is a SUBSTANCE, which means faith is TANGIBLE... it has value, it has worth.

The same scripture goes to say, faith is the EVIDENCE of things NOT seen... This is like an irony. How can what you haven't seen have evidence? But then in the Kingdom, BELIEVING is SEEING as against the world's concept of SEEING is BELIEVING. Little wonder why Mary said to the angel Gabriel, *"Behold the maidservant of the Lord! Let it be to me according to your word"* **[Luke 1:38].** And it happened!

My GO, Rev. Dr. Paul Jinadu puts it this way:

> Learn to praise God in the time of problems. Don't stop praising God because of the circumstances you are going through. Learn to walk through the valley.

That is a practical demonstration of faith in God Almighty.

The subject of FAITH is an all-important one as everyone needs a measure of faith in the journey of life. In fact, as earlier mentioned in the introductory part of the book, we all practice faith consciously or unconsciously at one point or the other.

Martin Luther King Jr describes better what FAITH is all about. According to him, "FAITH is taking the first step even when you don't see the whole staircase."

FAITH is the unseen reality. It sees what is not visible to the senses. It overrides every sense of logic and limitation. It is seeing the invisible enabling you to do the impossible. FAITH is seeing things with the eyes of God. It is because of FAITH that we are not conditioned by what our senses can rationalise. As we put our FAITH, confidence, and trust in God Almighty, we will have access to knowledge our natural senses or reasoning cannot have because FAITH overlooks impossibilities and rises above them.

FAITH is our foundation. The Bible says that it is by grace we were saved through FAITH, and this is not from ourselves, because it is the gift of God-not by works so that no one can boast **[Ephesians 2:8-10]**. Even though we were saved by grace, we still need to exercise FAITH to receive the salvation.

FAITH is the complete trust or confidence in someone. The closest that the Bible comes to offering an exact definition of FAITH is **Hebrews 11:1** just as I said earlier. It says,

> *"Now FAITH is the assurance of things hoped for, the conviction of things not seen."*

From this definition of FAITH in the Bible it can be said that the central feature of FAITH is confidence or trust.

FAITH is daring to do something regardless of the consequence based on your conviction. We sit on a chair because of the conviction we have that it will carry our weight. Based on our conviction, we buy our ticket and board the flight even though we are not familiar with the pilot nor care about his competence to fly. We also don't even bother about the state of fitness of the plane. We simply hope and believe that all will go well. We do things like this every time without thinking about it. We cannot count how many times we simply got into a car, bus, coach or a train to go on a journey, irrespective of the distance, without any effort to check on the fitness, and road worthiness of the vehicle. On many occasions, we don't even know or see the pilot or the train driver, yet we are comfortable to go on the journey. We just exercise faith and trust that everything will be fine. It baffles me when I hear people say they don't have faith, whereas we exercise faith to various degrees in our daily activities, based on the convictions we have.

We don't ever get offered a seat and the first instinct would be to check if the chair has the capacity or ability to carry our weight before we sit down. All these demonstrate that we practise faith in one way or another in our day-to-day life.

In fact, **Romans 12:3** says that God has given each of us a measure of FAITH. This means that we actually don't have a FAITH problem since God has already given to each one a measure of FAITH. What we have on the contrary is a FAITH activation problem.

FAITH is not a spare tyre we use when needed; when one of our tyres is deflated. No. FAITH is what we live by. FAITH is the spiritual air that sustains us. The Bible says that the just shall live by FAITH.

The importance of living by FAITH cannot be overemphasised. There are several scriptures in the Bible that tell us that our FAITH in God cannot be overstated.

One of such scripture is **Habakkuk 2:4**, it says:

> *"Look at the proud! They trust in themselves, and their lives are crooked; but the righteous will live by their FAITH."* **[NLT]**.

I will conclude this chapter by the words of Joel Beach. In his article titled, *Faith is not an assumption,* he writes;

True faith is to follow God without external assurances. It has no guardrails given by this world that man may grasp onto with his hands. It is walking upon the waters of belief in God's promises without visual proof that we won't sink. It is looking straight forward into the eyes of Jesus and stepping out upon the raging waters of the unknown with a joyful trust He will not allow you to fall—a knowing without seeing, believing without touching, and certainty without proof.

CHAPTER 2
GOD'S KIND OF FAITH

I am sure you would be wondering about the term 'God's kind of faith', perhaps you are thinking is God's faith different from the rest of us? The answer is indeed yes. God's kind of faith is different! In fact, there are two kinds of faith in a general sense.

There is "the God-kind of faith" and the "the human kind of faith."

The human-kind of faith is based on knowledge or information obtained from the senses. This type of faith calls real only those things that can be seen or touched physically. It doesn't produce any result; it gives you nothing. It's not true faith, because faith is the evidence of things not seen or perceived by the senses.

A good illustration of someone who operated in this kind of faith was Thomas, one of Jesus' disciples. When he heard that the Master had risen from the dead, he said,

"Except I see...I will not believe!" **[John 20:25]**.

Shortly afterwards, when Jesus showed up, He rebuked him saying,

"be not FAITHLESS, but believing..." **[John 20:27]**.

In other words, Thomas was faithless!

It therefore follows that those who say 'seeing is believing' are faithless according to the Scriptures. The human-kind of faith is no faith at all. It is zero-faith. I like to call it "the Thomas-kind of faith." Jesus went on to declare to Thomas,

"Blessed are they that have not seen and yet have believed" ***[John 20:29]***.

The blessed person is the one who believes before seeing.

This is the kind of faith that spoke the world into existence.

"Through faith we understand that the worlds were framed by the Word of God, so that things which are seen were not made of things which do appear" **[Hebrews 11:3]**.

How did He do it? God believed that what He said would come to pass. He spoke the Word and there was an earth. He spoke into existence the vegetable kingdom. He spoke into existence the animal kingdom. He spoke into existence the heavens as well as the earth, the moon, the sun, the stars and the universe. He said it and it was so. He believed what He said would come to pass and it did.

Then this brings us to the 'God kind of faith'! The best way I can explain God's kind of faith is that He creates things with His Word. He brings them into existence by merely speaking to them. **Hebrews 11:3** says:

- *By FAITH, we see the world called into existence by God's Word, what we see created by what we don't see. [MSG]*
- *By FAITH we understand that the entire universe was formed at God's command, that what we now see did not come from anything that can be seen. [NLT]*

In **Romans 4:17 [MSG]:**

We call Abraham "father" not because he got God's attention by living like a saint, but because God made something out of Abraham when he was a nobody. Isn't that what we've always read in Scripture, God saying to Abraham, "I set you up as father of many peoples"? Abraham was FIRST named "father" and then became a father because he dared to trust God to do what ONLY God could do: raise the dead to life; with a word, make something out of nothing. When EVERYTHING was HOPELESS, Abraham BELIEVED anyway, deciding to live not on the basis of what he saw he couldn't do but on what God said He would do. Hence, he was made father of a multitude of peoples. God himself said to him, "You're going to have a big family, Abraham!"

In Mark 11, we can see another illustration of God's kind of faith when Jesus cursed a fig tree that had no fruits on it. He said to the tree, *"No one is going to eat fruit from you again-ever!"* And His disciples overheard him. The next day when Jesus and His disciples passed by again, they found the tree dried up from the roots. Amazed, Peter said, *"Master, behold, the fig tree which thou cursed is withered away."*

It was then that Jesus made the statement in **Mark 11:22,** *"Have faith in God."* Another translation says, *"Have God's kind of faith."* The Message translation puts it this way: *"Embrace this God-life. Really embrace it."* After telling His disciples to have the God kind of faith, Jesus went on to explain in verse 23 what this meant: The God kind of faith is the kind of faith in which a man believes with his heart and says with his mouth that which he believes in his heart, and it comes to pass. Jesus showed that He had that kind of faith, for He believed that what He said would come to pass. He said to the tree, *"No man eat fruit of you hereafter for ever"*, and His disciples heard it [**Mark 11:14**].

Bill Winston in his book, 'the God kind of faith', writes that Faith unlocks a world of unlimited possibilities, connects you to the realm of the supernatural, and causes the unseen things (God's promises) to come into visibility. Jesus told His disciples, 'Have faith in God,' or you could say 'have or receive God's faith.' It's the same faith that God used to create the universe and every born-again believer has been given 'the measure' of it [**Romans 12:3**].

Jesus demonstrated the 'God kind of faith' to His disciples, and then He told them that they too had that kind of faith – the faith that a man believes with his heart, says with his mouth what he believes, and it comes to pass.

Someone might say, "I want that kind of faith. I am going to pray that God will give it to me." Well, you don't need to pray for it – you already have it.

> *"For I say, through the grace given unto me, to every man that is among you, not to think of himself more highly than he ought to think; but to think soberly, according as God hath dealt to every man the measure of faith"* [**Romans 12:3**].

Note that Paul wrote this to believers, for he says, "to every man that is among you." The epistle of Romans was not written to the sinners in the world; it was a letter to Christians. He addresses this letter "to all that be in Rome, beloved of God, called to be saints ..." [**Romans**

1:7]. And in it, he tells them that God has given to *every man the measure of faith."*

Yes, this is the absolute good news. We all have been given a measure of this kind of faith. In the Bible, the book of Romans further tells us that faith grows by hearing the Word of God. The more you hear the Word of God, the more real it becomes in your life and the easier it is to believe His promises.

Paul also said,

> *"For by grace are ye saved through faith; and that not of yourselves: it is the gift of God"* [Ephesians 2:8].

Paul is saying here that this faith is not of yourself. He was not referring to grace, for everyone knows that grace is of God. He is saying that the faith by which we are saved is not of ourselves. It is not a natural, human faith. It was given to sinners by God. And how did God give the sinner faith to be saved? **Romans 10:17** says, *"So then faith cometh by hearing, and hearing by the word of God."* In these verses Paul has said that faith (1) is given, (2) is dealt, and (3) cometh.

Romans 10:8 says,

> *"But what saith it? The word is nigh thee, even in thy mouth, and in thy heart: that is, the word of faith, which we preach."*

The Bible, this message of God, is called the word of faith. Why is it called the word of faith? Because it causes faith to come even into the heart of the unsaved. It causes the kind of faith that spoke the universe into existence to be dealt to our hearts. Faith is given to us through the Word.

God expects every believer to have this kind of Faith. In counselling sessions, I usually hear people tell me that they do not have faith, let alone

'God's kind of faith'. I beg to disagree! We all do. God has already given to us a measure of that 'kind of faith'. All we need to do is to activate it. Just the same way your bank sends you a new ATM card. It wouldn't work until it has been activated. Until it is activated, it is useless. Similarly, faith, though you have been given a measure, is useless until it is activated.

CHAPTER 3
A MEASURE OF FAITH

All born again Christians have been given a 'measure of Faith! If you are like me, perhaps you have wondered at the meaning of the term, 'a measure of faith'

In the English Standard Version of the Bible, **Romans 12:3** says,

> *"For by the grace given to me I say to everyone among you not to think of himself more highly than he ought to think, but to think with sober judgment, each according to the measure of faith that God has assigned."*

The New American Standard Bible, King James Version, and Holman Christian Standard Bible also contain "measure of faith," while "measure of faith" is presented as "the faith God has distributed to each of you" in the New International Version and "the faith God has given us" in the New Living Translation.

This simply means that we all have been given the same measure of faith. The very fact that it says the measure of faith, is indicative of the fact that it designates a quantity, or an amount. When you say, "measure," you think of a pint, or a gallon, or something you think of as a measurement, a quantity, or degree. So, when you say, "He dealt us the measure of faith," that means that we all start out with the same measure. Every person who accepts Christ as his or her personal Saviour has faith.

There are not different kinds of faith depending on who you are or the role you play in the Body of Christ. You may look at someone who seems to have strong, world-changing faith and think, "Gee, I'll never be like that person. That person is so confident and secure in his spiritual walk. That's not me."

This is not true! "The measure of faith" is the same for every believer, and it is the same faith that Jesus possessed. Different believers may have developed and strengthened their faith over time and by the Word, but their faith is no different than yours or mine. You have that same capability. Don't let anyone—fellow believers, the enemy or even your own mind convince you that you have weak or non – existent faith. That's a lie that, if you believe it, will keep you a weak, ineffective Christian. If you have become a new creation in Christ Jesus, then you have "the measure of faith." Like Jesus, your faith has the ability to move mountains. It simply needs to be exercised. But before we go into Faith activation or the exercise of faith, let's explore the different levels of faith in more detail.

The Bible has a lot to say about the different levels of faith. Christian faith is based on God's promises, rather than feelings, or things visible. Great faith holds fast regardless of outward appearances. No wonder **Romans 4:18-22** says,

> *"And being fully persuaded that, what he had promised, he was able also to perform."*

LEVELS OF FAITH

The Bible describes different categories or levels of faith. Each one of them is ascribed to different people based on how they exercise the faith they have.

1. **NO FAITH**: "Fearful, displaying a lack of total trust," was used by the Lord as a tender rebuke for anxiety and fear." In **Matthew 6:30**, Jesus said to the anxious ones, *"If God so clothes the grass of the field, which today is, and tomorrow is thrown into the oven, will He not much more clothe you, O you of little FAITH?"* In **Matthew 17:20**, Jesus talks about "little faith" while addressing the inability of His disciples to cure the sick child that was brought to them. He also talked of little faith in **Matthew 8:26**, *"You of little faith, why are you so afraid?"* Then He got up and rebuked the winds and the waves, and it was completely calm.

2. **FAILING FAITH**: We know that it is our faith that overcomes for us **[1 John 5:4].** Therefore, what the enemy is interested in is to cause our faith to fail us. Hence, when Satan asked to take Peter that he might sift him like wheat, Jesus assured him that He had already prayed for him so that his faith will not fail. It is possible for one's faith to also fail them.

3. **WEAK FAITH**: The "weak in faith" doesn't mean the person doesn't trust in Jesus as Saviour or that he is confused about the gospel. This faith believes for salvation but for little else. It believes God for eternity but not for anything else that can be obtained through faith. It only means they have refused to develop the muscle of faith. They are not condemned. As a matter of fact, **Romans 14:1-2** says, *"Welcome with open arms fellow believers who don't see things the way you do. And don't jump all over them every time they*

do or say something you don't agree with-even when it seems that they are strong on opinions but weak in the faith department. Remember, they have their own history to deal with. Some people's faith allows them to eat anything, but the person who is weak in the faith eats only vegetables." A person of weak FAITH will find limited opportunities to benefit from the Gospel, and very little of peace and joy that should accompany the Christian life. That is why **Romans 15:1** says, "We then who are strong ought to bear the infirmities of the weak, and not please ourselves." There is also provision for those who are weak in FAITH. The only thing is that they will not enjoy all the benefits they are entitled to as Christians. **Hebrews 6:12 [NIV]** says, "We do not want you to become lazy, but to imitate those who through FAITH and patience inherit what has been promised."

4. **WAVERING FAITH**: A wavering FAITH is an unstable FAITH. James encourages believers to put their FAITH into action. **James 1: 5-8 [AMP]** says, "If any of you is deficient in wisdom, let him ask of the giving God [Who gives] to everyone liberally and ungrudgingly, without reproaching or fault-finding, and it will be given him.' Only it must be in FAITH that he asks with no wavering (no hesitating, no doubting). For the one who wavers (hesitates, doubts) is like the billowing surge out at sea that is blown thither and tossed by the wind. For truly, let not such person imagine that he will receive anything [he asks for] from the Lord. [For being as he is] a man of two minds (hesitating dubious, irresolute), [he is] unstable and unreliable and uncertain about everything [he thinks, feels, decides]."

5. **GROWING FAITH**: FAITH is given to all to believe for salvation but can either remain at one level or can grow. This is evidenced in **2 Thessalonians 1:3 [NIV].** It says, "We ought always to thank God for you, brothers, and rightly so,

because your FAITH is growing more and more, and the love every one of you has for each other is increasing". The MSG translation puts it this way: *"You need to know friends, that thanking God over and over for you is not only a pleasure; it is a must. We have to do it. Your FAITH is growing phenomenally; your love for each other is developing wonderfully. Why, it's only right that we give thanks".* This shows clearly that love increases when FAITH grows because it is only then that one can see and act and love like God. Where there is acrimony and hatred; it is a clear demonstration of lack of FAITH. Just as nutritious milk helps a baby to grow strong and healthy; Spiritual food will help a baby Christian grow into a deeper level of FAITH. **1 Peter 2:1-3 [NLT]** shows us how we can grow our FAITH. "So, get rid of all malicious behaviour and deceit. Don't just pretend to be good! Be done with hypocrisy and jealousy and backstabbing. You must crave pure spiritual milk so that you can grow into the fullness of your salvation. Cry out for this nourishment as a baby cries for milk especially now that you have tasted of the Lord's kindness. We are not permitted to remain at one level of FAITH when we can grow in FAITH and enjoy our relationship with the Father better. As our FAITH grows, we resemble God more and we love even much more.

6. **FAITH WITHOUT WORKS**: FAITH without works passively believes and accepts the Bible literally, but without action. Many people fall into this category! They believe and have FAITH that God can do all His Word says. They believe in miracles yet fail to act on His Word. By acting on His Word, it means we must do whatever He says to do irrespective of how senseless that may seem. It means obeying His Word. **Isaiah 1:19 [MSG]** says, *"If you'll willingly obey, you will feast like kings."* In **1 Samuel**

15:22b-23 [NKJV], Samuel said, *"To obey is better than sacrifice, and to heed than the fat of rams. For rebellion is as the sin of witchcraft, and stubbornness is as iniquity and idolatry. Because you have rejected the Word of the Lord, He also has rejected you from being king."* When we refuse to act on God's Word by not activating our faith, we are already in disobedience and have rejected God Almighty. The consequence is rejection from Him too. In order not to be rejected by God we must act on His Word by FAITH and not reject His Word.

7. **STRONG FAITH**: **Romans 4:20** says that Abraham staggered not at the promise of God through unbelief; but was strong in FAITH, giving glory to God. When someone is strong in FAITH or has a strong FAITH, it means that it doesn't matter what the reality may look like, he still knows that God is able to do whatever He has promised to do. FAITH connects the Believer with the Power of God. The one who truly believes and has FAITH will act on God's Word with perfect assurance that his request will be granted.

8. **GREAT FAITH:** This is the kind of faith that holds fast regardless of outward appearances. The story of the Centurion whose servant was sick in **Matthew 8:5-10 [NIV]** is a great example. It records; *"When Jesus had entered Capernaum, a Centurion came to Him, asking for help. "Lord", he said, "my servant lies at home paralyzed and in terrible suffering." Jesus said to him, "I will go and heal him." The centurion replied, "Lord, I do not deserve to have You come under my roof. But just say the word, and my servant will be healed. For I am a man of authority, with soldiers under me. I tell this one, "Go," and he goes; and that one, "Come," and he comes. I say to my servant, "Do this," and he does it." When Jesus heard this, He was astonished and said*

to those following Him, "I tell you the truth, I have not found anyone in Israel with such great faith."

9. **IMMEASURABLE FAITH:** Paul wrote to the Thessalonian Church: *"Grace to you and peace from God our Father and the Lord Jesus Christ. We are bound to thank God always for you, brethren, as it is fitting, because your faith grows exceedingly, and the love of every one of you all abounds toward each other."* **[2 Thessalonians 1:2-3].** The Greek word for exceedingly, is *perissos*, which means immeasurable.

The above list is not exhaustive. There is another level of faith, *stubborn* or *violent* faith, which I will discuss in the next chapter. My plea is for us to take time out and reflect on these levels of faith, identify the category to which we fall into with the aim of growing our faith.

CHAPTER 4
STUBBORN FAITH

WHAT IS STUBBORN FAITH?

I believe that Stubborn faith as the Lord ministered to my spirit is another level of demonstration of our faith in Him. This is the level of faith that believes the Lord to do the unexpected and seemingly impossible before the eyes of man.

The difference between 'Stubborn Faith' and strong faith is that there may not have been any previous example to hold unto that God will do that impossible thing yet there is a conviction in your spirit man that whatever comes up the Lord will handle it. For strong faith, one can stand on and remind Him of what he did in the past and pray that He repeats that. For example, David in **1 Samuel 17: 34-37**, was able to declare boldly to King Saul that the Lord would deliver him from Goliath the same way He delivered him when he encountered the bear and the lion.

But Stubborn Faith is another dimension altogether. My experience in Pakistan on 24 October 2017 (an encounter which I will share in detail in subsequent pages) is a good example. I saw the move of God in a new dimension in my life. Prior to this, there was no experience or instance I could hold unto as a reference point that the Lord would come through in what was clearly an impossible situation in the sight of man. I believe my faith was strengthened when I was reminded by the devil (albeit in mockery) that I had just preached a sermon titled 'Stubborn Faith'. This was my wakeup call to exercise a "crazy" faith and trust God completely. Hence, rather than worry about what I was seeing (a lifeless man on the floor), I chose to hold unto the word I had received from the Lord earlier on at Qatar airport, "Stubborn Faith."

Dr. Kenneth Hagin once said,

> It doesn't matter what challenges I may be facing, all I do is locate God's promise/word concerning such a challenge and I hold onto that word. No matter the wind and no matter the storm, I won't let go of that word. I say to myself if I sink, this word will sink with me, and if I drown this word will drown with me. However, since I already know that God and His Word are the same, and that God cannot sink or drown it doesn't matter how fierce the wind or storm, I also know that I cannot sink PROVIDED I hold unto His Word.

This kind of faith can be likened to Stubborn Faith!

Stubborn FAITH will not waver at God's promises irrespective of the storm. A stubborn FAITH is unwavering. Believes without question. God says "jump" and he doesn't ask why, but only asks how high? It is sincere and unbendable. Stubborn FAITH is to count those things that be not as though they are **[Romans 4:17; Mark 11:22-24]**. It's the kind of faith captured in **Hebrews 10:23 [AMP]** which says,

> *"So, let us seize and hold fast and retain without wavering the hope we cherish and confess and our acknowledgement of it, for He Who promised is reliable (sure) and faithful to His Word".*

Stubborn Faith is FAITH in action. Even though the Bible says that we are saved by grace and not by works, **Ephesians 2:8-9** makes us know that Faith that is not actioned is dead. To capture it succinctly, FAITH without works is dead **[James 2:17-18]**. FAITH is dead when not exercised but comes alive when put in action; standing and acting on God's infallible Word.

In other words, FAITH must be demonstrated to make it acceptable and commendable. For instance, if I send my daughter on an errand, she knows she has my backing and that I will never abandon her to her own fate, therefore, despite the challenges that she may encounter on the way, she knows that I will watch over her until she gets back home. If I ask her to jump from a height with the assurance that I would catch her and not allow her to fall and hit her head on the floor, she will have no reason not to believe that I will do exactly what I promised. If she says she believes me but refuses to jump from that height simply because she feels I may not be able to hold her from hitting the floor, then she has no trust or FAITH in me, but if she jumps it is a demonstration of the FAITH she has in me.

The heart of man is terribly wicked according to **Jeremiah 17:9**, yet we are able to care for our children and do all we are able to prevent them from being hurt. **Luke 11:13** says it all, If you then, being evil, know how to give good gifts to your children, how much more will your heavenly Father give the Holy Spirit to those who ask Him. It therefore, means that if only we can exercise faith by trusting in God, then the scripture in **Isaiah 64:4** which says that 'since the beginning of the world men have not heard nor perceived by the ear, nor has the eye seen any God besides You, who acts for the one who waits for Him', will form an expression in our lives.

There are several scriptures to back up this viewpoint namely:

- **Nehemiah 4:14 [KJV]**: *"And I looked, and arose and said to the nobles, to the leaders, and to the rest of the people, "Do not be afraid of them. Remember the Lord, great and awesome, and fight for your brethren, your sons, your daughters, your wives, and your houses." Here the emphasis is "Remember the Lord."*

- **Jeremiah 1:17-19 [AMP]**: *"But you [Jeremiah], gird up your loins! Arise and tell them all that I command you. Do not be dismayed and break down at the sight of their faces, lest I confound you before them and permit you to be overcome. For I, behold, I have made you this day a fortified city and an iron pillar and bronze walls against the whole land-against the [successive] kings of Judah, against the princes, against its priests, and against the people of the land [giving you divine strength which no hostile power can overcome]. And they shall fight against you, but they shall not [finally] prevail against you, for I am with you, says the Lord, to deliver you.*

- **Nehemiah 4:14-15, 20 [AMP]**: *"I looked [them over] and rose up and said to the nobles and officials and the other people, "Do not be afraid of the enemy; [earnestly] remember the Lord and imprint Him [on your minds, great and terrible, and [take from Him courage to] fight for your brethren, your sons, your daughters, your wives, and your homes. And when our enemies heard that their plot was known to us and that God had frustrated their purpose, we all returned to the wall, everyone to his work. In whatever place you hear the sound of the trumpet, rally to us there. Our God will fight for us."* Note the emphasis here is also to *"Remember the Lord."*

- **Isaiah 43:1-5 [NLT]**: *"But now, O Israel, the Lord who created you says: "Do not be afraid, for I have ransomed you. I have called you by name; you are mine. When you go through deep waters and great trouble, I will be with you. When you go through rivers of difficulty, you will not drown! When you* *walk through fire of oppression, you will not be burned up; the flames will not consume you. For I am the Lord, your God, the Holy One of Israel, your Saviour. I gave Egypt, Ethiopia, and Seba as a ransom for your freedom. Others died that you might live. I traded their lives for yours because you are precious to me. You are honoured, and I love you. "Do not be afraid, for I am with you. I will gather you and your children from east and west".*

In **2 Chronicles 20:15b**, God says that the battle is not yours but His. All we need to do is to have FAITH in Him. If God be for us, who can be against us? Let us trust the Lord knowing that at the mention of the name of Jesus, every knee should bow and every tongue must confess that Jesus is Lord to the glory of God.

Demons tremble at His presence. **Psalm 18:44-47 [NLT]** says

"As soon as they hear of me, they submit; foreigners cringe before me. They all loose their courage and come trembling from their strongholds. The Lord lives! Blessed be my rock! May the God of my salvation be exalted! He is the God who pays back those who harm me; he subdues the nations under me."

The God who subdues nations under me, can subdue anything under me. All that I have been commanded to do is: "Fear not, only believe!"

I will also outline the Word of God in **Mark 5:36** in a few translations:

- *"Overhearing but ignoring what they said, Jesus said to the ruler of the synagogue, Do not be seized with alarm and struck with fear; only keep on believing."* **[AMP]**
- *"Jesus overheard what they were talking about and said to the leader, "Don't listen to them; just trust me."* **[MSG]**

The servants of Jairus had brought him the news that his daughter had been confirmed dead and that there was no need asking Jesus to come and heal the little girl. To them it was already too late. All that Jesus asked Jairus to do was to keep on trusting Him and we all know the end of that story! It does not matter what presents itself before us, the only thing that is required of us is to put our trust in Jesus.

PRACTICAL ACTIVATION OF FAITH

I have been faced with many seemingly impossible situations during my Christian journey and I have watched God come through in each of those instances. All it took was my staunch belief that God can do exceedingly abundantly above all I could ever ask or think. I followed this by being bold enough to take that RADICAL step of faith and trusting Him to come through on each occasion.

Find an account of just a few testimonies of faith activation below:

CHURCH BBQ on the 27th of August 2023

As part of our goals to look after people in our Community, my Church organises BBQ every year as part of our strategies for Evangelism. This is a function where we invite people to fellowship with us and this has proved to be an effective strategy for soul winning. On the last one we had (before writing the book), we had prepared for it lavishly as always. The Church service had ended just before 12.30pm so that everyone could go to the Church car park where we usually host the event to have fun. The Evangelism Team had also distributed flyers inviting people for the event.

Everything was ready and we were all looking forward to having a real good time, and I was counselling someone who had shared his personal problems with me inside the Church sanctuary. Just then, someone came to me to say, "Pastor Solution, it is raining; come and stop the rain." I did not think twice when I heard that. I stood up, went outside and started commanding the rain to stop. A lady who was passing by the church, said to me, "It is raining already." I said to her, "Yes, I can see but the rain will stop, madam."

I continued with my declarations; I went into the car park where the chairs that were arranged had already been soaked by the rain. I looked up into the sky and spoke to the rain. I said, "It is written that Elijah said that it will not rain except by his word, and the rain obeyed him." I commanded the rain to stop. By this time, my suit was already wet. I went back into the Church and someone gave me some tissue to wipe myself. I was still doing that when someone came from the car park to say to me, "Pastor the rain has stopped." This happened within a few minutes after I walked into the sanctuary. I was not surprised at the outcome, that was my expectation. May God's name alone be praised.

By the time I got back to the car park, I saw the same woman who was passing by, who had said to me that the rain had come anyway and that perhaps my prayers had come a little bit late. As she was hurrying home, she noticed that the rain had stopped and decided to come back and rejoice with the church. She told me that it was a huge surprise to her to see that the rain had suddenly stopped. That is what the exercise of our FAITH does to those who don't know Jesus. They start believing in our God. One of our senior ministers in the church, Mrs. Sade Akinola, told me a few days later that as soon as she heard someone call me to come and speak to the rain and I stood up, that she also stood up and came after me to the car park to see what would happen. That testimony also had a positive effect on her own FAITH.

~

LAHORE, PAKISTAN

Two outstanding testimonies are linked to this trip. I have attempted to share them below to strengthen our Faith and confirm the fact that God is always ready to meet with us if we trust Him enough to exercise our faith.

~

DEAD MAN COMES BACK TO LIFE

As I waited for my connecting flight from Qatar airport to Lahore, in Pakistan, I already had a minimum of fifteen messages I had prepared for the two- week long programme. As I was meditating and thinking of which message to kick off the programme, I heard the Holy Spirit say to me, "STUBBORN FAITH." Now, there was no such message among the ones I had ready, and my flight would be leaving in less than one hour. Moreover, the programme would kick off only a few hours after my arrival in Lahore. So, I had to quickly trust the Holy Spirit to help me before I got to Lahore. Remember I said earlier that if He gives the vision, He will also make the provision. On arrival at the airport in Lahore, my host, Pastor Andrew and his first son, picked me up and we went to his house.

Due to the time difference, (6 hours), I didn't really have enough rest before the programme started. The Church was in the same building, on the ground floor, while the room I lodged was on the last floor. Before one could say Jack Robinson, the service had started.

Being the first day of the programme, I thought it would be great to start with a message that will strengthen their faith so that as many people as possible would be able to grab their testimonies. That was exactly what I understood the title of the message meant. Nothing prepared me for what was to follow. I must have preached for over one hour and the service ended at about 10pm.

As people were leaving the church, a few young guys who could speak passable English were having a chat with me, when the Pastor came to me and said, "Pastor, there is trouble, they brought a dead man here." I asked him, "Dead man, where?" He pointed to a body on the floor at one side of the hall where we just had the service. The Pastor continued, "Pastor, some people were taking their sick relative to the hospital and he died in the car. When they saw the crowd coming out from the Church, they decided to bring the body into the Church." He said to me, "Pastor, they will claim that he came to Church where he died, and they might burn down the Church."

Apparently, the dead man was not a Christian. He belonged to another faith. Some of those who were already leaving the church, came back to see what was going to happen. My first feeling was fear obviously. If I knew where to run to, I would have done so. Anyway, a voice said to me, "Did you not just preach on stubborn faith just now?"

I walked across to where the body was, knelt down beside it and laid my hand on the man's forehead. All I said to the Lord was, "Father, if You raise this man from the dead, there will be real commotion in Lahore." Everybody was watching. Then I heard the devil say to me, "Mr. Stubborn Faith", to which I shouted, "Shut up!" and people heard it. Even though the weather was cold I was sweating, so I took off my jacket. After one hour, I tried to open the man's eyes but he did not blink, meaning he was dead. I closed his eyelids again and continued muttering words to the Lord. After another ten minutes or so, I opened his eyes again, and he blinked and sneezed. There was a loud shout. He was raised and positioned with his back beside the wall, and they gave him water to drink. His relatives who had been waiting outside, all came in. I picked up my phone and called my

Pastor, Rev. Tayo Arowojolu, without minding what time it was in the UK, and said to him, "Pastor, I have seen God at work", and narrated what just transpired. Pastor as usual, said "We thank God."

A BENT FOOT STRAIGHTENED

When I thought it was all over and just about to breathe a sigh of relief, I was presented with another seemingly impossible situation. A young man of about twenty four years stumbled up to me with his walking aid, a stick he had used for support for several years, and asked to be healed by Jesus. He was at the service earlier and was on his way out when he saw the people who brought in the dead body of the man. Out of curiosity, he changed his mind about leaving and came back inside the church like several others, just to see what would happen.

This young man's right leg was longer than the other because his left foot was bent at the knee. This left foot had never touched the ground since he was born. As I said, he had a long stick which aided his mobility. The moment he witnessed the miracle, he moved straight to me and pointed at his bent leg.

I just said to the Lord, "Father, how can this man who saw You raise the dead right under his nose and is trusting You to straighten his bent foot go home without his own miracle?" At this point, everyone was looking at us to see what would happen. My faith in God was again put to the test.

The first thing I did was to take away the walking stick from him. I asked the Pastor's wife, Pastor Margreth to hold the man on one hand while I gave him support on the other hand. At my direction, we made the first circle, then I asked Pastor Margreth to leave him. I was now holding him in one hand and we made another circle with only one of his legs touching the ground. As soon as we concluded that circle, I left him on his own and ordered him to repeat exactly what we did twice already; do a circle but this time alone. I assured him he would not fall. However, I was also watching him in case he tried to. As he obeyed and attempted to make the circle, his bent foot straightened and touched the ground. The commotion that followed was indescribable. There were shouts of Joy. This was indeed a creative power of God at work. Needless to say, many people surrendered their lives to Jesus. On Sunday, the man who the Lord had raised from the dead came to the church with one of his relatives and gave their lives to Jesus.

From this point, my stay in Lahore took a different turn as the many testimonies attracted people from far and wide. I was constantly busy, with very little or no sleep especially due to the time difference. As I mentioned earlier, there is a time difference of six hours; so when it is 6am in Pakistan, it would be 12 midnight in the UK, just when I would start feeling like catching a little sleep seeing I could not do so before that time. The Pastor would come and knock on my door and say to me, "Pastor, please come down to the church, people are waiting." Several people of other religion/s kept coming for prayers and giving their lives to Jesus to the extent that the Pastor became concerned that we could be attacked at the rate people were coming.

To ensure our safety, he arranged for services to be held in other locations apart from the church, such that we were not always at the same address for two consecutive prayer meetings. By the time we got to wherever the service was to hold, the place would be packed full. All this happened because I trusted the leading of the Holy Spirit and preached the message He gave me at Qatar airport, "STUBBORN FAITH."

Even today, whoever would dare to exercise stubborn faith will be amazed to see what God will do. Therefore, never lose hope even when the devil or your senses tell you it is over. By virtue of your stubborn faith, our God can send a miracle at any time. He is saying to someone reading this book, "Fear not only believe." Believe Him for whatever He has promised. Believe Him for that marriage. Trust Him for the fruit of the womb, irrespective of that doctor's report. He said that none shall be barren.

I decided to tell this story to show what stubborn faith can do even today. I still believe that when we put our stubborn faith to work, the Lord will do the impossible. Indeed, without faith we cannot please the Lord.

CHAPTER 5
IMPORTANCE OF FAITH

The importance of faith cannot be overstretched. Faith is the wheel on which we ride. With our faith unleashed in motion nothing shall be impossible to us. Our faith overcomes for us. **1 John 5:4b** says,

> *"This is the victory that overcomes the world, even our faith."*

Faith is what Satan is afraid of because he has no chance when we put our faith to work. No wonder, Jesus said to Simon Peter in **Luke 22:31 NKJV**:

> *"And the Lord said, "Simon, Simon! Indeed, Satan has asked for you, that he may sift you as wheat."*

Luke 22:32a in the Amplified version says,

> *"But I have prayed for you [Peter], that your {own} faith may not fail; and when you yourself have turned again, strengthen, and establish your brethren."*

I dare to say that Faith is such an important commodity that it is always the main target of the enemy. It is the trigger that releases the bullet from our gun. A gun with a jammed trigger cannot release its bullets no matter how many bullets the rifle may have.

Although, it is written in **2 Corinthians 1:20 [MSG]**:

> *Whatever God has promised gets stamped with the Yes of Jesus. In Him, this is what we preach and pray, the great Amen, God's Yes and our Yes together, gloriously evident.*

Our 'Yes' must agree with God's Yes for there to be a manifestation of His promises in our lives, and this is made effective through our faith. **Amos 3:3** says that two cannot work together unless they agree. After the messenger of God, Angel Gabriel spoke the word of God to Mary, her response was,

> *"Behold your handmaid, let it be unto me according to your word."*
> ***[Luke 1:38]***

Indeed our own YES to God's promises is very vital for there to be a manifestation.

One scripture that easily comes to mind to establish this truth is **Hebrews 4:1-7 [NKJV]**:

> *"Therefore, since a promise remains of entering His rest, let us fear lest any of you seem to come short of it. For indeed the Gospel was preached to us as well as to them; but the word which they heard DID NOT PROFIT THEM, NOT BEING MIXED WITH FAITH in those who heard it. For we who have believed do enter that rest, as He has said: "So I swore in My wrath, "They shall NOT enter My rest," although the works were finished from the foundation of the world. For He has spoken in a certain place of the seventh day in this way: "And*

God rested on the seventh day from all His works"; and again, in this place: "They shall NOT enter My rest." Since therefore it remains that SOME MUST enter it, and those to whom it was first preached did not enter because of DISOBEDIENCE, again He designates a certain day, saying in David, "Today," after such a long time, as it has been said: "Today, if you will hear His voice, Do not harden your hearts."

It is quite important to know that the fact that the promises are there doesn't guarantee that everyone must benefit from them. It will require mixing our faith with those promises for us to benefit from them. For this to take place, we must not harden our hearts. Salvation is the greatest of all miracles, given by grace and received by faith. The same way salvation is received by faith is the way every other promise of God should be received; BY FAITH.

Faith can change our circumstances for the better. Whatever the situation, our faith in the Lord is capable of changing the report. Four days after the death of Lazarus, Jesus went to his tomb and asked that the stone on the tomb be removed. Martha, the sister, said to Him, *"Lord, by this time the body must be stinking."* Jesus said to her in **John 11:40 AMP**:

"Did I not tell you and promise you that if you would believe and rely on Me, you would see the glory of God?"

The Book of **Hebrews 11:1-2 KJV** puts it this way:

"Now faith is the substance of things hoped for, the evidence of things not seen. For by it [FAITH], the elders obtained a good report."

You obtain a good report from a bad report, through faith.

To buttress the importance of faith, I will share a personal testimony involving my daughters. See the account below:

MY DAUGHTERS' TESTIMONIES

When my elder daughter, Favour was about 13 months old, we noticed that some part of her skin, around her thighs and her arms were a bit rough and those parts of her body were not responding to the creams we were using on her. A particular cream (EH40) or so, was prescribed for her skin and even though it wasn't cheap when compared with other creams, we made sure we always had extra for her at home. We took her to see a dermatologist who diagnosed her with eczema. He told us categorically that it was incurable, and she also said that she was just going to cope with it as there was nothing more they could do to help us medically. On hearing such an evil report, I told him categorically that my daughter was not going to live with that rough skin and that it would disappear. He kept on telling me that medically speaking it was not possible. Well, to the glory of God Almighty, the rough skin disappeared within only a matter of weeks without us applying any cream on her. I only kept declaring the promises of God over her without ceasing until the words became flesh and her healing became manifest.

That was not a one-off though. There was another incident, this time with the younger sister. She was a very active baby, fiercely independent and could walk at just seven months. Once she discovered the use of her legs, she loved to follow me around the house. One morning, as I came out of the bathroom to go into the bedroom to get ready to go to work, she was coming behind me but I didn't notice, maybe because I was rushing. The door to my room would always shut by itself. Not realising that she was right behind me, I didn't hold the door, so it slammed shut and her fingers got trapped in the door. I don't think I have heard any child cry the way she did. It was such a painful wail that broke my heart. One nail came off completely from one of her fingers as a result of the injury she sustained. When we took her to the hospital, they had an X-ray to ascertain that no bone was broken. Thankfully no bone was fractured.

The doctors told us that her nail will never grow back again because the nail bed was affected. I said to them audibly that her nails would grow. It was like an argument between us. About two or three doctors said that the nail would not grow, but I didn't take that from them. I told them that her nail would most definitely grow again. And I held firm to that belief without shaking, declaring every day that it would grow and believing God that it would be so. Within a period of weeks, the nail grew back perfectly. To this day, I can't tell which finger nail it was.

In the two testimonies shared above, all I did was exercise my faith and I obtained a good report from a bad one. That still works even today. Glory to God! The Book of **Ephesians 1:3 NIV** says,

> *"Praise be to God and Father of our Lord Jesus Christ, who has blessed us in the heavenly realms with EVERY spiritual blessing in Christ".*

It means that WHATEVER we need from God has been provided already in the spiritual realm. Faith is the currency we require to bring them to the physical realm.

From these accounts, it is a no-brainer that Faith is important. It is what can help us get through life when everything else hasn't worked and we are facing difficult times. Sometimes, it's all we have to hold on to during these times. In the case of my daughters above, Faith was all I had to hold on to! What else is there when the doctors themselves tell you that there is no hope? They are the professionals. They have been trained in that field and nobody can argue with them, or so it would seem. Not when I already know what the will of God is on the subject! Glory to God!!

Faith is an essential thing in life. It is the belief that things will work out despite the uncertainty of the future and good things will happen in the end. When you have done everything necessary you could to overcome a problem, utilising all your skills, knowledge, and resources, and getting help from everyone you know, and things still fail, faith is the remaining thing that can give you hope things will still work out.

In conclusion, Faith makes us stronger mentally. It awakens a sense spiritually that provides the assurance that we are not alone; we have a great God backing us and watching out for us. Faith provides a sense of purpose and direction in life and provides hope.

CHAPTER 6
EXPLOITS OF FAITH

When I think of people who have demonstrated stubborn FAITH, the first that easily comes to mind are the stories namely: The three Hebrew boys; Daniel; Mordecai; Paul and Silas and so many others. These are people who stood FOR THEIR faith, PUT THEIR LIVES ON THE LINE, AND THE Lord showed up for them. When you exercise your faith the Lord comes to your aid and your rescue because that is what pleases and moves Him to act on your behalf.

Hebrews 4:2-3 (NLT) says:

For this Good News—that God has prepared a place of rest—has been announced to us just as it was to them. But it did them no good because they didn't believe what God told them. For ONLY we who believe can enter His place of rest. As for those who didn't believe, God said, "In my anger I made a vow: "They will NEVER enter my place of rest, "even though His place of rest has been ready since He made the world."

We chose not to believe and act on God's word at our own detriment. No wonder Mary said to the disciples of Jesus in **John 2:5**, *"Whatever*

He says to you, DO IT."

He promised us in **Isaiah 43:2** that when we pass through the waters, He will be there and through the rivers, they shall not overflow us; when we walk through the fire, we shall not be burned; neither shall the flame kindle upon us. Hallelujah!

It was by faith in the name of the Lord that David approached and killed Goliath. He realised that what he was carrying inside of him was greater than the challenge he faced. This is the same with whoever will dare to exercise faith in what God says. **1 John 4:4** says that He that is inside us is greater than he that is in the world. As a matter of fact, David described Goliath as an uncircumcised Philistine. He didn't even bother to give him any form of recognition by giving him an appellation **(1 Samuel 17:26).** David understood that all he required to win was God's presence. **Romans 8:31** says, *"If God be for us who can be against us."* Jesus said that God is a Spirit **(John 4:24)**. He also said in **John 6:63** that the WORDS He speaks to us are spirit and they are life. In **John 14:6**, He says I am the life. In Revelations 19:13 it is written that His name is the Word of God. **Philippians 2:9-10** says that His name is above every other name and that at the mention of that name, Jesus, every knee should bow of things in heaven, and things on earth and things under the earth.

Once armed with the word of God concerning anything, we are good to go. Those who know that will do exploits **Daniel 11:32** says,

"Those who know their God shall be strong and do exploits."

THE THREE HEBREW BOYS: DANIEL 3:14-30 [MSG]

Nebuchadnezzar asked, "Is it true, Shadrach, Meshach, and Abednego, that you don't respect my gods and refuse to worship the gold statue that

I have set up? I'm giving you a second chance-but from now on, when the big band strikes up you must go to your knees and worship the statue I have made. If you don't worship it, you will be pitched into a roaring furnace, no question asked. Who is the god who can rescue you from my power? Shadrach, Meshach, and Abednego answered King Nebuchadnezzar, "Your threat means nothing to us. If you throw us in the fire, the God we serve can rescue us from your roaring furnace and anything else you might cook up, O King. But even if he doesn't, it wouldn't make a bit of difference, O King. We still wouldn't serve your gods or worship the gold statue you set up.

Nebuchadnezzar, his face purple with anger, cut off Shadrach, Meshach, and Abednego. He ordered the furnace fired up seven times hotter than usual. He ordered some strong men from the army to tie them up, hands and feet, and throw them into the roaring furnace. Shadrach, Meshach, and Abednego, bound hand and foot, fully dressed from head to toe, were pitched into the roaring fire. Because the king was in such a hurry and the furnace was so hot, flames from the furnace killed the men who carried Shadrach, Meshach, and Abednego to it, while the fire raged around Shadrach, Meshach, and Abednego.

Suddenly King Nebuchadnezzar jumped up in alarm and said, "Didn't we throw three men, bound hand and foot, into the fire? That's right, O King," they said. "But look!" he said. "I see four men, walking around freely in the fire, completely unharmed! And the fourth man looks like a son of the gods!" Nebuchadnezzar went to the door of the roaring furnace and called in, "Shadrach, Meshach, and Abednego, servants of the Highest God, come out here!" Shadrach, Meshach, and Abednego walked out of the fire.

All the important people, the government leaders and the king's counsellors, gathered around to examine them and discovered that the fire hadn't so much as touched the three men-not a hair singed, not a scorch mark on their clothes, not even the smell of fire on them!

Nebuchadnezzar said, "Blessed be the God of Shadrach, Meshach, and Abednego! He sent His angel and rescued his servants who TRUSTED (had FAITH) in Him! They ignored the king's orders and laid their bodies on the line rather than serve or worship any god but their own. "Therefore, I issue this decree: Anyone anywhere, of any race, colour or creed, who says anything against the God of Shadrach, Meshach, and Abednego, will be ripped to pieces, limb from limb, and their houses torn down. There has never been a god who can pull off a rescue like this." Then the king promoted Shadrach, Meshach, and Abednego in the province of Babylon.

~

DANIEL IN THE DEN OF LIONS: DANIEL 6:7-28 [MSG]

We've convened your vice-regents, governors, and all your leading officials, and have agreed that the king should issue the following decree: For the next thirty days no one is to pray to any god or mortal except you, O king. Anyone who disobeys will be thrown into the lion's den. "Issue this decree, O king, and make it unconditional, as if written in stone like all the laws of the Medes and the Persians." King Darius signed the decree. When Daniel learned that the decree had been signed and posted, he continued to pray just as he had always done. His house had windows in the upstairs that opened towards Jerusalem. Three times a day he knelt there in prayer, thanking and praising his God. The conspirators came and found him praying, asking God for help. They went straight to the king and reminded him of the royal decree that he had signed. "Did you not, "they said, "sign a decree forbidding anyone to pray to any god or man except you for the next thirty days? And anyone caught doing it would be thrown into the lion's den? Absolutely," said the king. "Written in stone, like all the laws of the Medes and Persians." Then they said, "Daniel, one of the Jewish exiles, ignores you, O king, and defies your decree. Three times a day he prays." At this, the king was very upset and tried his best to get Daniel out of the fix he'd put him in. He worked at it the whole day long. But then the conspirators were back; "Remember, O king, it's the law of the Medes and Persians that the king's decree can never be changed." The king caved in and ordered Daniel brought and thrown into the lion's den. But he said to Daniel, "Your God, to whom you are so loyal, is going to get you out of this." A stone slab was placed over the opening of the den.

The king sealed the cover with his signet ring and the signet rings of all his nobles, fixing Daniel's fate. The king then went back to his palace. He refused supper. He couldn't sleep. He spent the night fasting. At daybreak the king got up and hurried to the lion's den. As he approached the den, he called out anxiously, "Daniel, servant of the living God, has your God, whom you serve so loyally, saved you from the lions?" "O king, live forever!" said Daniel. "My God sent His angel, who closed the mouths of the lions so that they would not hurt me. I've been found innocent before God and also before you, O king. I've done nothing to harm you." When the king heard these words, he was happy. He ordered Daniel taken up out of the den. When he was hauled up, there wasn't a scratch on him. He had trusted God. (He had a STUB-BORN FAITH in God.)

Then the king commanded that the conspirators who had informed on Daniel be thrown into the lion's den, along with their wives and children. Before they hit the floor, the lions had them in their jaws, tearing them to pieces. King Darius published this proclamation to every race, colour, and creed on earth: Peace to you! Abundant peace! I decree that Daniel's God shall be worshipped and feared in all parts of my kingdom. He is the living God, world without end. His kingdom never falls. His rule continues eternally. He is a Saviour and a Rescuer. He performs astonishing miracles in heaven and on earth. He saved

Daniel from the power of the lions. From then on, Daniel was treated well during the reign of Darius, and also in the following reign of Cyrus the Persian."

~

When your FAITH is stubborn and radical, it will not only save you from troubles, but will also encourage other people to believe in and have FAITH in your God, as we can see in the cases of both the three Hebrew boys, Shadrach, Meshach, and Abednego, and that of Daniel. In both cases, two different kings decreed that the God of the Jews was to be worshipped by all because He alone is the Living and true God. God looked at their stubborn FAITH and made the opposite of the plans of their enemies to occur.

Now we can see why it is written in the Book of **Esther 9:1[NKJV]**:

" Now in the twelfth month, that is, the month of Adar, on the thirteenth day, the time came for the king's command and his decree to be executed. On the day that the enemies of the Jews had hoped to overpower them, the opposite occurred, in that the Jews overpowered those who hated them".

He will always be lifted above every other god wherever He sees FAITH in action. Jesus made it clear in the Book of **John 12:32** that if He be lifted up from the earth, He will draw all men unto Himself. If we can lift His name up in FAITH while going through challenges of life, He sure will pull us up out of the mess.

That is why the Bible says in the Book of **Hebrews 13:15 [AMP]**,

"Through Him, therefore, let us CONSTANTLY and at ALL times offer up to God a SACRIFICE of praise, which is the fruit of lips that thankfully acknowledge and confess and glorify His name."

We don't go by what we feel, but by what we believe. Whether our body feels like it or not, we should bring praise to Him as a sacrifice. By doing so we invite Him into our ugly situation and His presence will make the difference we desire to see. The Bible says that He inhabits the praises of His people **[Psalm 22:3]**. In His presence there is fullness of joy and at His right side there are pleasures for ever more **[Psalm 16:11]**. Most importantly, His presence causes mountains and hills to melt and dissolve like wax **[Psalm 97:5]**.

In **Isaiah 43:21,** we know that the reason why we were formed is so we might praise Him. The [MSG] translation puts it this way:

> *"The people I made especially for Myself, a people custom-made to praise Me."*

The only reason God formed us is so that we can sing His praise, and only a person who has FAITH can praise God during challenges. FAITH makes you say to yourself that since God is the beginning and the end, He is also in the middle therefore is always in control, and you are able to sing His praises even in the midst of the storm. The Word of God says in **Romans 12:12 [AMP],**

> *"Rejoice and exult in hope; be steadfast and patient in suffering and tribulation; be constant in prayer."*

We are to live in hope and we are to rejoice. After all, FAITH is the substance of that which we hope for. So, when Satan comes to steal your victory and tell you that God doesn't care about you, you just think on the Word of God and start rejoicing, knowing that greater is He that is in you than He that is in the world. Brag on God rather than complain or murmur. The devil can't stand it at all. You can be steadfast and patient in suffering. Tribulation means "being under pressure." That is not the time to cave in. When things get hard isn't when you let go of the Word. That is when to double up on it, so that you are immovable. This is a demonstration of your FAITH in the faithful God Who has called you.

It is a demonstration of FAITH when we can praise Him during challenges. We must learn to lay down our pride, our wisdom, our feelings, and our pains to worship Him. Below are a few of my favourite songs whenever I am faced with difficult times.

Song One:

O be lifted, above other gods,
we lay our crowns and worship You.
O glorious God, we praise Your name,
we lay our crowns and worship You.

Song Two:

We clap our hands in the sanctuary.
We clap our hands to give you the glory.
We clap our hands to give you the praise,
And we will praise You for the REST of our days.

Song Three:

I will sing of the mercies of the Lord forever;
I will sing of the mercies of the Lord!
With my mouth, will I proclaim,
Your FAITHFULNESS, Your FAITHFULNESS,
With my mouth, will I proclaim,
Your FAITHFULNESS, to all generations.

Song Four:

No matter what I'm facing,
when trouble comes my way,
I will praise the Lord.

The ability to praise Him no matter what we are facing is what I call a demonstration of FAITH. It is faith that will cause one to sing.

PAUL AND SILAS – ACTS 16:19-34 [MSG]

"When her owners saw that their lucrative little business was suddenly bankrupt, they went after Paul and Silas, roughed them up and dragged them into the market square. Then the Police arrested them and pulled them into a court with the accusation, "These men are disturbing the peace-dangerous Jewish agitators subverting our Roman law and order."

By this time the crowd had turned into a restless mob out for blood. The judges went along with the mob, had Paul and Silas's clothes ripped off and ordered a public beating. After beating them black and blue, they threw them into jail, telling the jailkeeper to put them under heavy guard so there would be no chance of escape. He did just that, threw them into the maximum-security cell in the jail and clamped leg irons on them.

About midnight, Paul and Silas were at prayer and singing a ROBUST hymn to God. The other prisoners couldn't believe their ears. Then, without warning, a huge earthquake! The jailhouse tottered, every door flew open, all the prisoners were loose. Startled from sleep, the jailer saw all the doors swinging loose on their hinges. Assuming that all the prisoners had escaped, he pulled out his sword and was about to do himself in, figuring he was as good as dead anyway, when Paul stopped him: "Don't do that! We're all still here! Nobody's run away!"

The jailer got a touch and ran inside. Badly shaken, he collapsed in front of Paul and Silas. He led them out of jail and asked, "Sirs, what do I have to do to be saved, to really live?" They said, "Put your ENTIRE trust in the Master Jesus. Then you'll live as you were meant to live- and everyone in your house included!" They went on to spell out in detail the story of the Master-the entire family got in on this part. They never did go to bed that night. The jailer made them feel at home, dressed their wounds, and then-he couldn't wait till morning! -was baptised, he and everyone in his family".

The exercise of your FAITH does more than save you from danger; it also gives other people who witness your testimony the opportunity and the confidence to put their own ENTIRE trust in the Lord. The Lord always looks after His Word to perform it. He promised in **Isaiah 43:2, NLT**,

"When you go through deep waters and great trouble, I will be with you. When you go through rivers of difficulty, you will not drown! When you walk through the fire of oppression, you will not be burned up; the flames will not consume you."

BLIND BARTIMAEUS: MARK 10:46-52 [NLT]

"And so they reached Jericho. Later, as Jesus and his disciples left town, a great crowd was following. A blind beggar named Bartimaeus (son of Timaeus) was sitting beside the road as Jesus was going by. When Bartimaeus heard that Jesus from Nazareth was nearby, he began to shout out, "Jesus, Son of David, have mercy on me!"

"Be quiet!" some of the people yelled at him. But he only shouted louder, "Son of David, have mercy on me!" When Jesus heard him, He stopped and said, "Tell him to come here." So they called the blind man. "Cheer up," they said. "Come on, He's calling you." Bartimaeus threw aside his coat, jumped up, and came to Jesus. "What do you want me to do for you?" Jesus asked. "Teacher," the blind man said, "I want to see!" And Jesus said to him, "Go your way. Your faith has healed you. "And instantly the blind man could see! Then he followed Jesus down the road."

This is the story of a blind man who sat by the roadside begging for alms. But when he heard that Jesus was passing, he started calling on Jesus to have mercy on him and restore his sight. Those whose eyes were "open" (but could not see that Jesus's mission on earth was and is still to open the eyes of the blind among other things), tried to discourage him by saying that Jesus didn't have the time to waste on people like him. However, the more they tried to discourage him, the louder he shouted to get the Lord's attention until Jesus, seeing such demonstration of faith, stopped and asked those around to go and call him. I always prefer to say that Jesus turned the blind man's mockers into his messengers. Jesus could have walked towards the blind man but chose to use the same people who tried to silence the blind man as his errand men.

Nothing in the physical showed that his sight could be restored, yet he stubbornly believed that Jesus had the power to open his eyes. He knew exactly what he wanted and he had faith for it. All he needed to do was release his faith to receive what he needed. He did not allow other people's opinion/s to influence his choice and his resolve to receive his healing from Jesus to Whom ALL powers belong. He was determined to not let the opportunity pass him by.

In what way have you allowed other people's opinions to limit you from pushing forward to receive your own miracle or your own testimony? Have you been told that because of one reason or the other you cannot get that job, that spouse, that healing, that breakthrough? Don't forget that opinions are like noses, it is useful only to the owner. God has not given you any limits so you cannot allow other people's opinion to limit you. They did all that they could to stop Bartimaeus from receiving his sight, but he chose to put his faith to work and that was what attracted Jesus's attention. Jesus is no respecter of persons. He will stop to attend to whoever will release their stubborn faith today. Glory to God!

THE WOMAN WITH THE ISSUE OF BLOOD: MARK 5:25-34 [NLT]

And there was a woman in the crowd who had had a haemorrhage for twelve years. She had suffered a great deal from many doctors through the years and had spent everything she had to pay them, but she had gotten no better. In fact, she was worse. She had heard about Jesus, so she came up behind him through the crowd and touched the fringe of His robe. For she thought to herself, "If I can just touch His clothing, I will be healed." Immediately the bleeding stopped, and she could feel that she had been healed! Jesus realised at once that healing power had gone out from Him, so He turned around in the crowd and asked, "Who touched my clothes?" His disciples said to Him, "All this crowd is pressing around You. How can You ask, "Who touched Me?" But He kept on looking around to see who had done it. Then the frightened woman, trembling at the realisation of what had happened to her, came and fell at His feet and told Him what she had done. And He said to her, "Daughter, your faith has made you well. Go in peace. You have been healed."

This story is another demonstration of what stubborn faith looks like. The woman had suffered for twelve long years and had spent her money in the hands of doctors and herbalists and instead of her health improving, she got worse. She settled it in her mind that what God cannot do does not exist. **Matthew 19:26** actually says that what is impossible with men is possible with God. So, after spending all her money she then realised that there is a 'Doctor' that does not charge money to heal. Suddenly, she came to the realisation that the only money she needed to give in exchange for her healing was her faith. She realised that healing is the children's bread. It is written that our FAITH is the victory that overcomes the world for us **1 John 5:4**. You cannot win if you don't have faith. Even though **1 Peter 2:24** says that we were healed by His stripes, we also must of course receive the manifestation of this healing by releasing our faith.

THE FAITH OF A GENTILE WOMAN: MATTHEW 15:21-28 [NLT]

Jesus then left Galilee and went north to the region of Tyre and Sidon. A Gentile woman who lived there came to him, pleading, "Have mercy on me, O Lord, Son of David! For my daughter has a demon in her, and it is severely tormenting her." But Jesus gave her no reply-not even a word. Then His disciples urged Him to send her away. "Tell her to leave," they said. "She is bothering us with all her begging." Then He said to the woman, "I was sent only to help the people of Israel—God's lost sheep-not the Gentiles." But she came and worshipped Him and pleaded again, "Lord, help me." "It isn't right to take food from the children and throw it to the dogs," He said, "Yes, Lord," she replied, "but even dogs are permitted to eat crumbs that fall beneath their master's table." "Woman," Jesus said to her, "your FAITH is GREAT. Your request is granted." And her daughter was instantly healed.

MARK 7:25-30 [NIV]

In fact, as soon as she heard about Him, a woman whose little daughter was possessed by an evil spirit came and fell at His feet. The woman was a Greek, born in Syrian Phoenicia. She begged Jesus to drive the demon out of her daughter. "First let the children eat all they want," He told her, "for it is not right to take the children's bread and toss it to their dogs." Yes, Lord," she replied, "but even the dogs under the table eat the children's crumbs." The He told her, "For such a reply, you may go; the demon has left your daughter." She went home and found her child lying on the bed, and the demon was gone.

From the above two scriptures, you will agree with me that this woman in question got what she wasn't qualified for or entitled to, but her "STUBBORN FAITH" received it for her. Jesus Christ, our Lord will do the same thing for WHOEVER would dare to believe Him because He is no respecter of persons.

MY CLASSMATE IN SECONDARY SCHOOL – HENRY

One of my classmates in Secondary School, Henry by name, was a very handsome young man who loved the Lord from a very young age. He was always neatly dressed in his school uniform. His life exuded peace from all the pores of his skin. But Henry wasn't a man cut for boyfriend and girlfriend life. As a matter of fact, Henry would always say to me and a few of our other classmates who were misbehaving then believing we were the "happening" at the time, "Lammy Heeler" (my nickname at the time), there is a life far better than what you think is that which you people call "life." He would always want to preach to us and we would make mockery of him as a "juu man" (a derogatory word we used to address all those who were not living like us, the "guy men"). Henry loved Jesus so much that when we left Secondary School, he went to work at the Christian Missionary Society, CMS Christian Bookshop where he would have the opportunity to study his Bible and preach Jesus to customers who came into the bookshop.

He had rich parents too, so leaving for the United States of America for further studies eventually was what we all knew would happen someday. On graduation, he got married to a beautiful girl who was also a staunch Christian herself. His parents travelled to America for the wedding ceremony. A few months after their beautiful wedding while everyone was expecting pregnancy to show up, his newly wedded wife took ill and the doctors gave them the bad news that except her womb was removed, there was no way her life could be saved. And what that meant was "goodbye to any hope of becoming proud parents of their own children". Henry didn't think twice about it when faced with the challenge. After he consented to the surgery that took out his wife's womb, he was glad that his wife was safe.

Typical of African parents, mothers in particular, Henry came under a lot of pressure from his parents to marry a second wife or divorce the wife. Henry staunchly refused. The parents then pressured him to pay off the wife (settle her financially) so he can be free to remarry since he refused to marry a second wife. Henry told the parents that marriage was "For better and for worse". Out of sheer anger and to make him pay, as he was their only child and should be the only one to inherit their estate, the parents hurriedly prepared their will and did not include him in their will.

But Henry refused to budge. He trusted God absolutely, always believing that God has the power to give them children. In the end, the wife got pregnant and had a baby against all odds! Henry travelled back to the same doctors in the United States who performed the operation, and they were dumbfounded. That is what our God can do in the face of unwavering faith as that exhibited by Henry. This is called, Stubborn Faith.

THE TWO BLIND MEN HEALED: MATTHEW 9:27-30 [MSG]

As Jesus left the house, He was followed by two blind men crying out, "Mercy, Son of David! Mercy on us!" When Jesus got home, the blind men went in with Him. Jesus said to them, "Do you really believe I can do this?" They said, "Why, yes, Master!" He touched their eyes and said, "Become what you believe." It happened. They saw. Then Jesus became very stern. "Don't let a soul know how this happened." But they were hardly out the door before they started blabbing it to everyone they met.

Once your demonstration of stubborn faith brings you results, nobody prompts you to do the work of an evangelist. That just comes naturally to you as you want others to come and taste and see that the Lord is good. Your faith grows even much stronger.

RAISING OF JAIRUS' DAUGHTER: MARK 5:22-42

A ruler of the Synagogue named Jairus had come to ask Jesus to come to his house to heal his only child, his daughter, who was very sick so that she might live and not die. Jesus obviously accepted and was going with him when suddenly the woman with the issue of blood intercepted Him and delayed His movement. As the woman with the issue of blood received her own miracle and testimony, the servants of Jairus came to tell their boss, Jairus that it was needless bothering Jesus because his child was dead already. Apparently, they thought it was already too late for any miracle to take place.

Mark 5:35 [AMP] says, *While He was still speaking, there came some from the ruler's house, who said [to Jairus], your daughter has died. Why bother and distress the Teacher any further?*

Mark 5:36 [AMP] – *"Overhearing but ignoring what they said, Jesus said to the ruler of the synagogue, Do not be seized with alarm and struck with fear; only keep on believing."*

At this point, Jairus had an option to continue to believe or say to the Master, "I came to You while she was still breathing but you allowed Yourself to be delayed by the woman with the issue of blood even though I came to you before her, what can You do now that it is too late? He would have gone home to bury his daughter. However, he chose to believe and continued to believe, even though prior to that he may never have heard that Jesus raised any one from the dead.

Mark 5:38-42 [AMP]:

"When they arrived at the house of the ruler of the synagogue, He looked [carefully and with understanding] at {the} tumult and the people weeping and wailing loudly. And when He had gone in, He said to them, Why do you make an uproar and weep? The little girl is not dead but is sleeping. And they laughed and jeered at Him. But He put them all out, and, taking the child's father and mother and those who were with Him, He went in where the little girl was lying. Gripping her [firmly by the hand, He said to her, Talitha cumi–which translated is, Little girl, I say to you arise [from the sleep of death]! And instantly the girl got up and started walking around–for she was twelve years old. And they were utterly astonished and overcome with amazement."

Truly God is waiting for anyone who dares to trust Him to do whatever seems impossible for them. These two blind men said to Him that they believed He could make them see. Their circumstance did not deter them from believing Him for the impossible.

What is it that you think is impossible for our Lord and Saviour, Jesus to handle? Are you able to release your faith right now for Him to work with?

The Bible tells us why we should be persistent when asking the Lord for anything whatsoever. It can only be through the exercise of our faith. The way we show that we trust God is by our resolve and determination never to give up irrespective of how the times may look. Someone said that "Winners never quit and quitters never win." The Book of **Proverbs 24:10** sums it up succinctly;

> *"If you faint in the day of adversity, your strength is small."*

It means that FAINT is evidence of lack of FAITH. Those who have FAITH will not FAINT.

Daniel 11:32b buttresses this point:

> *"Those who know their God shall be strong and do exploits."*

We can only know God when we spend time with Him and not give up despite the situation. This means we will continue to rely and depend on Him trusting Him to show up nonetheless. After all, the story of Lazarus who was in the tomb for four days and was brought back to life further demonstrates that no time is too late for Jesus to perform a miracle.

We need to be intentional about trusting God and in exercising our faith just like the story of the widow in **Luke 18:1-8 [NKJV]**. It says,

> *"Then He spoke a parable to them, that men always ought to pray and not loose heart, saying, there was in a city a judge, which feared not God, nor regard man. Now there was a widow in that city; and she came to him, saying, "Get justice for me from my adversary. And he*

would not for a while; but afterward he said within himself, "Though I do not fear God nor regard man, yet because this widow troubles me I will avenge her, lest by her continual coming she weary me." Then the Lord said, "Hear what the unjust judge said. And shall God not avenge His own elect who cry out day and night to Him, though He bears long with them? I tell you that He will avenge them speedily. Nevertheless, when the Son of Man comes, will He find FAITH on the earth?"

What Jesus is saying here is that your faith is required when you come to Him for anything.

There are so many scriptures in the Bible that give the confirmation that the proof or demonstration of faith and trust in God is in not giving up on Him because He will never give up on us.

One of such scriptures is **Isaiah 62: 6-7**:

"I've posted watchmen on your walls, Jerusalem. Day and night they keep at it, praying, calling out, reminding God to remember. They are to give Him no peace until He does what He said, until He makes Jerusalem famous as the City of Praise". **[MSG]**

God says in **Isaiah 43:26 [AMP]**:

Put Me in remembrance [remind Me of your merits]; let us plead and argue together. Set forth your case, that you may be justified (proved right).

In **Isaiah 41:21** the Bible says:

"Present your case," says the Lord. "Bring forth your strong reasons," says the King of Jacob **[NKJV]**

The Lord Jesus whenever He was faced with any situation always said, "It is written." In other words, He was reminding God the Father of His promises concerning that situation.

The reason why some people faint when faced with situations could be either because they are ignorant of what the will of God is concerning such a situation, or they don't put God in remembrance of His word.

Even though angels are so powerful (one angel killed 185,000 people in one night [2 Kings 19:35], and they (angels) are at our service according to Hebrews 1:14, their ears are fashioned to hear only the voice of His Word.

Psalm 103:20 says,

> *"Bless the Lord, you His angels, who excel in strength, who do His word, heeding the voice of His word"* [NKJV]

The angels are like "waiters" in a restaurant. They don't bring anything to you until you place an order. When we enforce God's word by speaking and believing it, the angels run with it and deliver to us. Afterall, the Bible makes it very clear in Ephesians 1:3, that our blessings are in heavenly places. When we remind God of His promises and remain immovable and unshakeable, the angels bring the blessings down to us.

Little wonder why one of God's Generals, Kenneth Hagin of blessed memory said,

> There is a corresponding solution in the Bible to every problem in life. Therefore, once I locate the solution in the word of God to any challenge I may be passing through, I hold onto that word from God and I keep saying to myself, "It doesn't matter the wind and it does not matter the storm, I will not go off this word. If I have to sink this

word will sink with me, and if I have to drown, this word will drown with me. I know that God and His word are one and the same, and I know that God cannot sink or drown, therefore if I hold unto His word, I will not drown.

This, brethren, is what I call, "STUBBORN FAITH."

In order that we may understand the role our faith plays in all this; the Bible elucidates further in the Book of James how to deploy faith when asking anything of the Father — **James 1:5-8 [AMP]:**

> *"If any of you is deficient in wisdom, let him ask of the giving God {Who gives} to everyone liberally and ungrudgingly, without reproaching or fault-finding, and it will be given him. Only it must be in FAITH that he asks with no wavering (no hesitating, no doubting). For the one who wavers (hesitates, doubts) is like the billowing surge out at sea that is blown hither and thither and tossed by the wind. For truly, let not such a person imagine that he will receive anything [he asks for] from the Lord. [For being as he is] a man of two minds (hesitating, dubious, irresolute), [he is] unstable and unreliable and uncertain about everything [he thinks, feels, decides]".*

This means that our faith in God should be unshakeable irrespective of how the situation looks like. We cannot look at the situation instead of looking on Jesus Christ. Our faith must be radical.

ABRAHAM'S FAITH

We cannot talk of stubborn faith without mentioning Abraham. Let's look at **Romans 4:16-25 [AMP]**

> *"Therefore, [inheriting] the promise is the outcome of FAITH and depends [entirely] on FAITH, in order that it might be given as an act*

of grace (unmerited favour), to make it stable and valid and guaranteed to all his descendants- not only to the devotees and adherents of the Law, but also to those who share the FAITH of Abraham, who is [thus] the father of us all.

As it is written, I have made you the father of many nations. [He was appointed our father] in sight of God in Whom he believed, Who gives life to the dead and speaks of the non-existent things that [He has foretold and promised] as if they already existed.[For Abraham, human reason for] hope being gone, hoped in FAITH that he should become the father of many nations, as he had been promised, So [numberless] shall your descendants be.

He did not weaken in FAITH when he considered the [utter] impotence of his own body, which was as good as dead because he was about a hundred years old, or [when he considered] the barrenness of Sarah's [deadened] womb. No unbelief or distrust made him waver (doubtingly question) concerning the promise of God but grew strong and was empowered by FAITH as he gave praise and glory to God, Fully satisfied and assured that God was able and mighty to keep His word and to do what He had promised.

That is why his FAITH was credited to him as righteousness (right standing with God). But [the words], it was credited to him, were written not for his sake alone

But [they were written] for our sake too. [Righteousness, standing acceptable to God] will be granted and credited to us also who believe in (trust in, adhere to, and rely on) God, Who raised Jesus our Lord from the dead, Who was betrayed and put to death because of our misdeeds and was raised to secure our justification (our acquittal), [making our account balance and absolving us from all guilt before God].

The confirmation that God will do for us through our faith what He did for Abraham who received through faith is in **Galatians 3:29 [NLT]**.

"And now that you belong to Christ, you are the true children of Abraham. You are his heirs, and now all the promises God gave to him belong to you".

The fact that Abraham appropriated those promises through his faith means that to receive those same promises we need to activate our own faith. In fact, faith is what we give in exchange to receive those promises. God is no respecter of persons **[Acts 10:34]**. Praise God!

FAITH IS VISIBLE AND CAN BE SEEN

Let's look at **Mark 2:1-5 [NKJV]**:

> "And Jesus having returned to Capernaum, after some days it was rumoured about that He was in the house (probably Peter's). Immediately many gathered together, so that there was no longer room to receive them, not even near the door. And He preached the word to them. Then they came to Him bringing a paralytic who was carried by four men. And when they could not come near Him because of the crowd, they uncovered the roof where He was. So, when they had broken through, they let down the bed on which the paralytic was lying. When Jesus SAW THEIR FAITH, He said to the paralytic, "Son, your sins are forgiven you."

If you have faith in God, it will be visible to others when you go through issues of life. It is not enough to say you have faith if your faith cannot be seen by other people.

I remember a certain incident that occurred at one of our 'Elders' Meeting in Church shortly after we had acquired our own property where we currently have as our place of worship. Each time we talked about the mortgage; the treasurer, a gentleman to the core, a Christian with a heart of gold, who always means well, would look at the amount of money that we had in our account. He would look at the tithes and offerings that were coming in from the church meetings and would take time at the meetings to explain how things were not looking good. Each time, he would say "there is no money", and that we would struggle to pay our mortgage for a particular period.

This was always the case and obviously we struggled somehow with the mortgage payment. There was even a time when the Pastor wasn't around and his associate then, Rev. Dr. Femi Idowu, (now gone to be with the Lord), summoned the Elders after a Sunday service, to an emergency meeting and asked everyone to URGENTLY lend some money to the Church, and that the money was required same day, so we could meet up with the quarterly payment of our mortgage that was to go out from the Church account on the Tuesday, and the money would be refunded to us the moment the church accounts looked better. We all did, each one as he could. The mortgage went through and we did not default. At the next Elders' Meeting, when the financial report was presented to us and the treasurer ended his presentation with, "there is no money" (which was a fact though), the lead Pastor, Rev. Tayo Arowojolu, blurted out, "from today I don't want to hear that there is no money again". We cannot be confessing each time that there is no money and expect a different result. He said, "there is money." "We have money". That was a demonstration of some stubborn faith there. Since that meeting, several years later, we have never used that phrase "there is no money" ever again and we have never struggled with repaying our mortgage.

The church finances miraculously took a turn for the better just because the Pastor chose to believe. His faith was seen. Can your own faith be seen by others? If that is not the case, I challenge you from now to make it seen. Until your faith can be seen you are not walking by faith.

HEALING OF TEN LEPERS: LUKE 17:12 -14 [AMP]

And as He was going into one village, He was met by ten lepers, who stood at a distance. And they raised up their voices and called, Jesus, Master, take pity and have mercy on us! And when He saw them, He said to them, Go [at once] and show yourselves to the priests. And as they went, they were cured and made clean.

By law, lepers were not meant to go into the city. Their place was at the entrance of the city, or what we can call the City Gate. Leprosy was considered a taboo sickness, a curse, yet, because they had faith in the word Jesus spoke, they acted on the word and immediately they were healed. Faith responds with action. That is why the Bible says that faith without works is dead.

When Jesus says jump, all we should ask is "How high?" Faith sees ahead.

CHAPTER 7
FAITH AT WORK

God is a specialist in dealing with impossibilities. When God says a thing, He watches over His Word to fulfil it (**Jeremiah 1:12**). All that is required from you is to have faith in Him. I have experienced God's goodness and miraculous breakthroughs in seemingly impossible situations in the course of my ministerial life. The main reason I feel led to share these testimonies is to help build up your faith.

Below are a few more testimonies:

JANGO'S WIFE IN BOMBAY, INDIA

I was living in Bombay (now Mumbai) in India, in an area called Colaba, where the world-famous Taj Mahal hotel is situated. Majority of the tourists from all over the world who visit Bombay, lodge in some not too expensive hotels around there, also because hard drugs were not difficult to come by in that area. Being an addict myself at the time, I couldn't have lived in any other area in Bombay except the Colaba area.

I had an Indian friend, Jango by name, who spoke very good English. He had lived abroad for several years before he came back to live in Bombay.

He was a motor mechanic by profession, but unfortunately had also been gripped by the spirit of drug addiction, and in order to fuel the habit, had also started dealing drugs himself. He had a wife and three beautiful children, two girls and one boy. We were quite close such that I could go to his house at any time, no matter how late, to get my supply whenever I needed drugs. Most of the time, we would stay together in my own hotel room to consume our crack cocaine and heroin since he didn't always use the drugs in the presence of his family inside their one-room apartment.

On this day, I had gone to him to get my supply as I had only woken up from sleep and due to the withdrawal effect of drugs, my body craved for immediate use of heroin. So I went to his place, rang the doorbell, and one of the children opened the door for me. As I stepped inside the room, I saw the children were crying and their mum was also weeping. When I asked what the problem was, I was told that their mum, Jango's wife who had been on admission in one of the hospitals due to ill health, was discharged by the doctors, was sent home and was given the bad news that she had only three more days to live.

Understandably, everyone was sad. She said to me, "Solution, who will look after my little children?" I was confused. When I asked after my friend, I was told he had gone out to inform relatives (there were no mobile phones at the time), so that they could plan to attend his wife's funeral which was to take place within three days' time. India is a very big country and people come from very far regions to reside in the State of Maharashtra whose capital is Bombay (now Mumbai). So, there was need to inform relatives in time so they could plan to attend her 'funeral' since doctors had pronounced her death sentence. In their own words, the illness had progressed so badly that there was no hope for her.

While I was still standing there not knowing what to say, my eyes went straight to a Bible on the table. I asked the lady, "Are you Christians?" She said, "Yes we are." I had visited that house so many times for at least two years and never knew what religion they belonged. Majority of the people were Hindus though and I assumed that they too were of the Hindu religion. I walked to the table, picked up the Bible and didn't really know what to do. I remembered the story I was told as a child that Prophet Elijah in the Bible used salt to heal something or somebody. I didn't really know where that was in the Bible. Even though my body craved for heroin, I couldn't walk out to purchase the drug from another dealer. So, I asked one of the children to put water in a cup and give me a little salt which she did. I placed the Bible on the cup and said a simple prayer, "O God, please, even though Indian doctors are known all over the world to be good and always almost correct in their predictions, instead of this woman living for just three days, keep her for four days or more so the doctors' would have gotten their prediction wrong for once, Amen."

I gave her the water to drink and I left. I went back to my room without stopping to buy my heroin from anyone else. I got on my bed and slept throughout the day until evening. On waking up, I decided to go back to my friend's house to buy the heroin. I had completely forgotten about my friend's wife. When I knocked on their door and the door was opened for me, to my greatest amazement, I saw the woman busy preparing dinner.

The moment she saw me, she said, "Solution, I will not die. As soon as you left after I drank the water you prayed over, I knew I wasn't going to die." My friend, Jango, was just there gazing into the sky, thinking of how he was going to look after three children alone. When she finished preparing dinner, we all ate, and I returned home thanking God for showing up for that family. On the third day (the day that she was supposed to die), their relatives began to arrive for the 'funeral'. Each time someone knocked on the door she would go and open the door for them by herself. You could see the shock on the faces of those who believed they were coming for her funeral.

Two weeks after the date she was supposed to have been buried, she returned to the same hospital, to the same doctors who were all surprised that she was still alive. They conducted a series of tests on her and confirmed that she was completely healed. They said it was a miracle. Indeed, faith works wonders. God healed her even when I was not serious with my Christian walk. Our God is indeed a wonderful God. I exercised my measure of faith and He did the rest. God exalts His Word above all His names.

～

THE HEALING OF BRAIN HAEMORRHAGE IN LONDON

It was about 1 am on that fateful night when I received a call from a member of my Church, New Covenant Church, Edmonton, in London, informing me that her father was rushed to the Queen Elizabeth 2 Hospital in Woolwich on his 70th birthday for brain haemorrhage and requested that I stand with the family in prayers for God to heal him. Rather than just pray over the phone, I told her I was coming to the hospital immediately. My wife, Stella, decided to accompany me to the hospital. I sent a text message to my Pastor informing him of what was happening and promised to keep him updated each step of the way.

On arrival at the hospital at about an hour or so after we spoke on the phone I met the lady and her husband with her other siblings and spouses standing with some doctors anxiously waiting for good news from somewhere. Beside where they stood, was a bed on which their father was, with all the tubes and other gadgets from life-saving machine/s to keep him alive while the doctors awaited the reply from the "best" brain surgeon in the UK, to whom a scan of his brain had been sent. Outside was an air ambulance to convey him to Kings College Hospital, where the "brain expert" was working should he say there is any chance of survival. However, if he looked at the scan and said it was too late for him to try to salvage the situation, they would not take him there. Should that be the case, he would just be left to expire gradually. The atmosphere in the hospital room was tensed up as we all sat there waiting for the test results to come back. From time to time, a doctor went to look at the computer screen to see whether the expert had replied. At one point he shook his head and said, "Guys, I just have bad news for you. The expert said that nothing can be done for your father." As soon as he said that, some of the children and their spouses began to cry uncontrollably. I almost started to console them for their loss.

At that moment, it was as if the Holy Spirit whispered to me, "Did you come all this way just to hear the doctors' report and go home?" I moved towards the bed where the man was laid, and I placed my hand on a part of his body where I could find a space (nearly all parts of his body had one tube or gadget from the several machines around him). I prayed to God Almighty to perform a miracle. I didn't pray for up to ten minutes or so and went back to where the rest of the people and my wife were standing and I said to them, "Let's just trust God." One of the doctors asked me, "what did you just do?". I told him I prayed for the man's miraculous healing. He asked me whether I had heard that the BEST brain surgeon in the UK had said there was nothing to do for the man. I said to him, "That is his own opinion, and that the Doctor of doctors had not said there was nothing He could do for the man." He said to me, "You people are just fanatics."

When we left, my wife told me that while I laid my hand on the man and prayed, the machines shook so hard and there were strange noises. She asked me if I noticed that and I told her that I didn't notice as I normally shut my eyes anytime I am praying. As usual, I sent a text message to my Pastor that I had prayed and that I was on my way home. That must have been about 5.30am. We got home at about 7am and I slept. When I woke up at about 11am, I got a text message from one of the man's daughters saying, "Thank God, daddy pulled through the night." I replied to her, "We thank God." At about 5pm the same day, she called me and shouted, "Pastor Solution, Miracle, Miracle." I said to her, "Share it." She said, "Daddy woke up and said he was hungry. They've taken him out of the ICU (Intensive Care Unit), into a normal ward and he is even eating food now as I am talking to you."

I also screamed joyfully and called my Pastor immediately to relay the good news to him, after which I drove straight to the hospital.

On arrival at the hospital, having been informed of his new location, I asked and was shown the place. His sister who was sitting at his bedside, said to him, "this is the Pastor who came to pray for you."

The man was looking almost fully recovered, he was free of all the machines and even sat up on the bed. He said to me, "Pastor, thank you for saving my life." I replied, "Sir, it wasn't me. It was Jesus that healed you" (**Acts 9:34**)

How I wish I could meet that same doctor who called me a fanatic for trusting Jesus to perform miracles!! It would be very interesting to hear what he would have to say.

~

GOD HEALED A WOMAN WITH A MENTAL ISSUE IN LONDON

It was on the 4th of May 2005, I was at Dalston market in London with my uncle's wife, Mrs. Comfort Ego Oji. We were shopping for a surprise birthday party which was scheduled for the following day, 05/05/05. I left her in one shop and walked into another one to ask for something that we couldn't find where we both were, while she picked up a few items we needed from there. The moment I got into that next shop, I saw a woman begging for food (corn cake) from the shop owner, while the shop owner kept telling her to leave her shop. So, I said to the shop owner to give her what she wanted and that I was going to pay. The woman said to me that the lady also had some outstanding debts with her, and I told her I would pay. When she gave the food to the lady and asked her to leave her shop, she also asked for sardine she would use to eat the food she just collected. The shop owner cursed her, telling her, "You greedy fellow, someone just paid for your food and cleared you old debts and you are asking for sardine." I told her to give her sardine and paid. Just at that moment, my uncle's wife walked into the shop where I was and saw this lady. She held me and screamed, saying, "I can't believe this, I can't believe this, this is sister Patience!!." She told me she knew the woman from a very long time, and that several years before then, the woman used to drive them in her car to go to my town association meetings.

I was shocked! Little did I know that the woman I showed kindness to, was from my own town in Nigeria. What a small world! At that point, I said to my uncle's wife, "We cannot continue shopping." I remember saying to her, "Who knows if the Lord brought us to this very shop so we could meet this lady! (**Esther 4:14**). I decided to take the woman to my church so we could pray for her.

So, we took her to the church bus, helped her inside and drove to New Covenant Church, Edmonton branch which at the time was situated at 800a High Road, Tottenham. I prayed for her and after the session asked for her address and took her home to Clapton. When we got into her house, it was very unkempt; it looked like it had not been cleaned for years. I handed her my complimentary card before I left.

A few days later, I got a voicemail from someone asking me to please kindly return her call which I did. She happened to be a nurse in the Mental Hospital at Homerton Hospital. Apparently, when I left the lady on that day, she left her apartment and wandered out to the streets where the Police saw her and took her to the hospital in Homerton. When this nurse found my card on her she called me because she had faith that prayers would help her better than the medications.

So, I rushed to the hospital where I was allowed to take her into one of the rooms and pray for her. I gave her a copy of a new Bible. Two days later, she called my phone and said that she was given two hours to go outside and come back as her condition had dramatically improved. She went to visit a friend of hers, Mercy by name. She said that when her friend saw her, she asked her how she got well.

Apparently, her friend knew she had developed mental issues that had degenerated over time. When she told her friend that one Pastor prayed for her, her friend asked if I could come and pray for her also. When I gave my consent that I would come to pray for her friend the following day, as I was engaged on that day, her friend gave me the address where she lived in Hackney. (I will share Mercy's testimony next.)

The Bible says in **Hebrews 13:2 [NLT]**,

> *"Don't forget to show hospitality to strangers, for some who have done this have entertained angels without realising it!"*

I showed this woman kindness without knowing that she was from not just my town but also from my very village. We even share the same surname, yet we never knew each other. Furthermore, in the Book of **Esther 4:14b [AMP],** Mordecai said to Esther,

"And who knows but that you have come to the kingdom for such a time as this and for this very occasion?"

God does not waste His resources at all. Wherever we find ourselves at any given time we should express our faith that expresses itself through love. I am very happy to share that this woman is well to this day almost two decades after, and still comes to my Church. All thanks to God.

～

MIRACULOUS HEALING IN LONDON – MADAM MERCY

After Sister Patience connected me to her friend on the phone, Mercy and I agreed I would come and pray for her the following day, I told my Pastor about it. I always told him about my movements for two simple reasons. First and foremost, I inform him of my movements so he could back me up in prayers, and secondly because I was in the Church employ at the time and it was quite normal that he should know where I was in case he needed me.

When my satnav, (Tom-Tom) directed me to her area and said I had arrived at my destination, it was a "No Entry", zone and I couldn't leave the church van on the road (the traffic wardens would plant a parking ticket on the van if left unmanned), so I called her phone. It was a landline; the same one she had given to me the day sister

Patience called me from her place. When I called and told her my predicament, she asked me to stay in my vehicle and that she was coming to get me. Not knowing what her ailment was at the time, I had hoped she would arrive within a few minutes as I was almost close to her house. It was just the 'no entry' sign that prevented my access. I waited and waited with no sign of her until I became impatient. So, I started calling her phone but she was not picking up. I must have called her number at least twenty times and she did not pick. I was determined to drive off, having waited for almost one hour in the van.

Luckily, I had to call the Pastor to tell him what was happening and that I was going to leave. Thank God for wisdom, he said to me, "Solution, don't leave. You've driven that distance and waited this long. Just be praying in the van and keep trying her line. At least I know your whereabouts." I thanked him and continued praying in the car. A few moments later, I looked outside the van, and there stood a woman with a Zimmer frame looking towards my van. I asked her, "Madam, are you Mercy?" She said to me that she was the one. To say that my mind nearly left me would be an understatement because I had thought the person I was coming to pray for could be needing a breakthrough in marriage, job, or her papers, or fruit of the womb. Nothing ever made me imagine that I was coming to pray for someone who couldn't walk.

The first thing I whispered to the Lord was, "Lord, how do I explain to this woman that You can heal madness but cannot heal lameness?" I said, "Lord, please show up and have mercy on sister Mercy." I came down from the vehicle, walked across the road to help bring her into my van. To bring her across the road to the van was not an easy task because she was quite frail. She felt a weakness from her waist down. There was no strength there. It must have taken us ten minutes to do that. Now another task was to help her into the van. The church van is quite high, and I was all alone. Once we were inside the van, she then guided me how to get into her street from another side. When we parked in front of her house, I also managed to get her down and we went into her sitting room.

For another hour she was narrating to me the genesis of her problem, and how spiritual bullets were shot into her waist on a particular morning she was at work doing her cleaning job. Prior to that she had been stranded in Nigeria for over a year where she was deported by the Immigration Services even though she had all her five children in the UK. In Nigeria, everyone avoided her because they all claimed that a bad omen was following her wherever she went. One Pastor who took her in with his family after hearing her sad story and had compassion on her, also sent her away for the same reason until a group of solicitors in the UK took up her case, fought for her and she was allowed to return to the UK.

On arrival from Nigeria, her husband suddenly didn't want to have anything to do with her anymore, even though he was the one who contacted the Citizen Advisory Bureau who organised the solicitors who fought for his wife to come back into the country.

The Council provided her a temporary accommodation and the cleaning job. According to her, she was just on the second week on that job when spiritual bullets were shot into her waist and she fell down and couldn't get up.

She was rushed by an ambulance to Homerton Hospital where several scientific tests were run but nothing was detected, and yet she couldn't walk. After a long time in hospital, she was discharged and the hospital provided her with a Zimmer frame to enable her move around her flat since it was obvious they couldn't help her! A care plan was drawn up for her and carers assigned to help her round the clock, meaning she was expected to remain like that possibly for the rest of her life.

When her story got too long for me, I said to her, "Madam, don't worry, the Lord knows the rest and He also knows what He alone would do." **John 6:6** assures us that Jesus always knows what He will do. He is never confused. Hallelujah!

I started by singing songs of Praise and Worship to charge up the atmosphere. The easiest way to bring in the presence of God is by praising and worshipping Him irrespective of the situation. The Bible says in the Book of **Psalms 22:3**, that The Lord inhabits the praises of His people. His presence makes hills melt like wax **[Psalm 97:5]**. There are so many scriptures in the Bible that show what praises can do. For example, **2 Chronicles 20:22 NKJV** says,

> *"Now when they began to sing and to praise, the Lord set ambushes against the people of Ammon, Moab, and Mount Seir, who had come against Judah, and they were defeated."*

No power can stand against praises and worship. Unfortunately, the human mind wants to look at the problem rather than focus on the SOLUTION, Jesus Christ, whose presence is easily invited through praise and worship.

As usual with me, I can be easily distracted, hence I always close my eyes whenever I am worshipping, praising or praying. I had scarcely sung for ten minutes, hadn't even started praying, when the lady shouted, "Pastor, I feel something, I feel something." Sensing that the Lord had performed a miracle on her, I said to her, "If you felt something, why not remove your hands from the Zimmer frame?" She took her hands off the aid and started jumping, for the first time in two years. I took out my phone and called my Pastor and I said to him, "Pastor, I have seen God at work again." When I left her, I went straight to my Pastor's office. As I was on my way back from her house, I was calling her line to check up on her but she was not picking and I was concerned. I kept on calling her throughout the day until she picked. When I enquired from her why she was not picking my calls, she told me that as soon as I left her house, she went out to show herself to people around, knocking on doors of her neighbours and going from one shop to another in her neighbourhood.

People started calling my number from all over because her testimony went wide. As a matter of fact, she shared her testimony in one of the services at New Covenant Church, Edmonton, where the Zimmer frame was taken from her and dumped inside a waste bin by the church.

HEALING OF HIV/AIDS PATIENT IN LONDON

A few years ago, I was in Victoria, London visiting my cousin, Uchechi, when I got a call from an unknown number. The caller said his name was Harry, a Nigerian, and was presently on admission in a hospital. He had been diagnosed with HIV/AIDS and the sickness was now at a very critical state. In fact, his case was a hopeless one as the Doctors just informed him, he had only three days more to live.

When he told me the verdict from the Doctors, I told him that the Lord was able to heal any sickness or disease and I began to pray for him (**Psalm 103:1-5**). He interrupted the prayers and requested I come down to see him in person at North Middlesex Hospital in North London, which was nearly 90 minutes' drive from where I was at Victoria. I excused myself from the cousin I had gone to visit and headed straight to the hospital.

On arrival, I saw a man who death was obviously staring in the face. He was bones only, his face and eyes portrayed someone who had practically lost hope. There on the little chair beside the bed where he was, was a Bible. He was inconsolable. It is difficult to imagine what could have been going through the mind of someone who was told by doctors that he had not more than ninety-six hours to live.

To compound his pain, his own wife abandoned him in the hospital and would not even bring their only child to the hospital to bid farewell to him. He was crying. I asked him a very simple question if he trusted Jesus to heal him despite the doctors' report, to which he muttered, "Pastor, I believe." I prayed for him and asked the Lord to prove the doctors wrong again. After I prayed for him, a nurse who was apparently positioned to monitor him, asked me whether I understood that the doctors had said that he would not survive beyond three days, to which I replied, "That is their own opinion and not the Lord's.

He survived and has shared his testimony each time he came to our Church until I pleaded with him to stop as he made it appear as though I was responsible for his healing. He is now a Pastor in another Pentecostal Church in London, and through him I met another great servant of God who is one of his relatives back in Nigeria. I was privileged to meet his parents before they both passed on to glory. The most interesting thing about this testimony is that some of the hospital workers who knew him while he was in their custody waiting for him to breathe his last, starting from the Nigerian nurse who I met the very first time and who told me that even the prayers came too late, gave their lives to Jesus Christ.

In appreciation of the members of the Evangelism Team of New Covenant Church, Edmonton, I would mention here that after my first encounter with this patient at the hospital, I came back and narrated the whole episode to them. We all contributed money, got in touch with the wife and daughter, paid them visits while the man was in hospital and followed them up until he was discharged from the hospital completely healed. I pray the Lord's blessings on you all, and you know yourselves. May He remember you for good. From Sister Tope Adeniyi, Sister Rachael Chirimutal, Sister Joy Esieme, Sister Alvanis Ijomanta, Brother Seyi Osibodu, Pastor Chuks Nnah, Brother Steve Kpalobi, Sister Gbemi to mention just a few of the brethren. I also want to thank those of you who have become part of the Evangelism Team thereafter. You've all been amazing and the Lord will remember you for good. Your reward will surely come in your lifetime for being part of this testimony. [**Revelations 22:12** and **Hebrews 6:10**].

TESTIMONY OF A SOLICITOR AT WALTHAM CROSS, LONDON

As I said earlier, Mercy's testimony went very far and my phone didn't stop ringing as a result. One day in 2007, I got a call from a lady who after introducing herself, told me that she could not sleep in her flat due to the strange noises she was hearing at night. I asked her to send me her address. I called my Church member then, who now pastor's our Cheshunt branch, Pastor Victor Olatunji, who lives in the same area to accompany me. When we arrived at the address, pressed her doorbell and she let us into her flat, we exchanged pleasantries. I left her and Pastor Victor in the sitting room and went into her bedroom, kitchen and toilet, made prophetic declarations and gave the demons operating there, quit notice to vacate the flat, relying on the authority Jesus gave to me in **Luke 10:19** and **John 14:12**, which say that I have been empowered to do exactly what Jesus would do in the circumstance.

Luke 10:19 –

- *"Behold! I have given you authority and power to trample upon serpents and scorpions, and [physical and mental strength and ability] over all the power that the enemy [possesses]; and nothing shall in any way harm you."* [**AMP**]
- *"Behold, I give you the authority to trample on serpents and scorpions, and over all the power of the enemy, and nothing shall by any means hurt you."* [**NKJV**]

John 14:12 –

- *"I assure you, most solemnly I tell you, if anyone steadfastly believes in Me, he will himself be able to do the things that I do; and he will do even greater things than these, because I go to the Father."* **[AMP]**
- *"The person who trusts me will not only do what I'm doing but even greater things, because I, on my way to the Father, am giving you the same work to do that I've been doing. You can count on it."* [**MSG**]

What this simply implies is that we are counting on the integrity of His Word rather than on our wisdom, or power. All we need to do is to believe Him and put our faith to work. Simple!

The prayers and prophetic declarations didn't last more than ten minutes, and we were done. The lady asked me if that was it, and I told her she would sleep like a baby that night and we left her house. The next morning, she called me excitedly and said, "Pastor, I slept even on my sofa and overslept." To me it didn't come as a surprise. That was my expectation to the glory of God. The Word of God says in **Psalm 18:44-45**,

> *"As soon as they hear of Me they shall obey Me, and the strangers will submit themselves and come off from wherever they are hiding."*

I gave a quit notice to the demons operating in her life and they obeyed.

Then she continued, "Please, there is something I didn't tell you last night, because I wanted to see if the first problem would be resolved." When I asked her to go ahead, she said to me, "Pastor, I am forty years old and have never been proposed to, despite the fact that I have been in relationships in the past." At that point, I asked her to come meet me in the church. We agreed on the time and I sent her the address. When she arrived, I said to her that before anything, we needed to go through the scriptures to ascertain that what she was desiring and wanted us to pray about is in the will of God, based on **1 John 5:14-15**, seeing that God hears only prayers according to His will.

1 John 5:14-15 AMP and NLT:

And this is the confidence (the assurance, the privilege of boldness) which we have in Him: [we are sure] that if we ask anything (make any request) according to His will (in agreement with His own plan), He listens to and hears us. And if (since) we [positively] know that He listens to us in whatever we ask, we also know [with settled and absolute knowledge] that we have [granted us as our present possessions] the requests made of Him. [**AMP**]

And we can be confident that He will listen to us whenever we ask Him for anything in line with His will. And if we know He is listening when we make our requests, we can be sure that He will give us what we ask for. [**NLT**]

It is quite important to know the will of God about anything even before we start praying about it in order not to pray amiss. So, we looked into the Scriptures to find out what God's infallible word says concerning marriage in the first place.

For instance, on marriage, we found the following:

Genesis 2:18-24 [NLT]

And the Lord God said, "It is not good for the man to be alone. I will make a companion who will help him." So the Lord God formed from the soil every kind of animal and bird. He brought them to Adam to see what he would call them, and Adam chose a name for each one. He gave names to all the livestock, birds, and wild animals. But still there was no companion suitable for him. So the Lord caused Adam to fall into a deep sleep. He took one of Adam's ribs and closed up the place from which he had taken it. Then, the Lord God made a woman from the rib and brought her to Adam. "At last!" Adam exclaimed. "She is part of my own flesh and bone! She will be called "woman", because she was taken out of man." This explains why a man leaves father and mother and is joined to his wife, and the two are united into one.

Proverbs 18:22 [NLT]:

The man who finds a wife finds a treasure and receives favour from the Lord.

Standing therefore on these scriptures, I knew that God will hear because it is in His plan; it is His will. Then we prayed and I enforced God's sentence based on **Acts 15:19 [KJV]** and commanded every obstacle and roadblocks to her being located by and married by her own husband to be removed. **Isaiah 57:14 NKJV** says,

"And, one will say, "heap it up! Heap it up! Prepare the way. Take the stumbling block out of the way of My people."

The NIV says, *"Remove the obstacles out of the way of my people."*

So, whether the obstacles or stumbling blocks were spiritual or physical, I stood on God's word and commanded them to be removed from her way.

She told me she was working with a Law Firm somewhere around Tottenham Hale in North London. A little while after our prayers, she called to tell me that a friend of hers in Jamaica sent her a link to apply for a position that might interest her and that she had done so. A few weeks later, she called to say that she had been offered the position but was reluctant to take up the offer. I said to her that this God we serve works in mysterious ways. Then I added, "Do you know whether that is where the husband we prayed about will find you?" She replied, "Pastor, I have travelled to Jamaica several times." I said to her, "My sister, even Hannah went to Shiloh several times, but a particular one was different from the previous ones." She then agreed to go to Jamaica to take up the job. After reaching an agreement with her boss (Principal), she left for Jamaica to take up the job.

That must have been around August 2007. By December, I travelled to Nigeria. I was with my mum, my wife and other relatives in my compound in Arochukwu when I received a call on my UK line. It was not a number I was familiar with so I decided to pick the call. (It is quite costly to answer calls on my UK line abroad). When I picked the call and realised she was the one, I told her I was in Nigeria and couldn't stay on the phone for long due to the roaming cost. She said, "Pastor, please don't drop. I met a man and he is serious. He has even proposed to me and this is the first time in my life. We are getting married in a few months from now." Three months later, they wedded in Jamaica and a few more months after the wedding her contract ended. She then had to come back to the UK and back with the previous Firm she was working with and started preparations to get her husband to join her here. So, it appears that the Jamaica opportunity was solely for her to meet her husband. Our God sure works in mysterious ways.

Back at work, her boss (Principal) wanted to get rid of her. He was always finding faults with her performance at work. One day she called to inform me that the guy said she should stop working with the Firm, and when she asked for the money due her, she was told that any other time she would mention that he would show her that he is a

Yoruba man from Nigeria. I told her to open her Bible and read James Chapter five and verse four for me.

- **James 5:4 [MSG]:** *All the workers you've exploited and cheated cry out for judgement. The groans of the workers you used and abused are a roar in the ears of the Master Avenger.*
- **James 5:4 [NIV]:** *Look! The wages you failed to pay the workmen who mowed your fields are crying out against you. The cries of the harvesters have reached the ears of the Lord Almighty.*

Now it is clear why the Bible says in **Colossians 4:1 [AMP]:**

Masters, [on your part] deal with your slaves justly and fairly, knowing that also you have a Master in heaven.

I advised her to believe in God and His word and see what will happen. I said to her that the word I received from God Almighty when He came into my prison cell on 21st March 2001, was, **Romans 10:11**, which summarises the Scripture. It says:

No man who believes in Him [who adheres to, relies on, trusts in Him] will [ever] be put to shame or be disappointed. **[AMP]**

I advised her to look for another job and never call or visit the boss ever again. She heeded my advice and got another job. God says in **Psalm 46:10** [AMP]: Let be and be still and know (recognise and understand) that I am God. I will be exalted among the nations! I will be exalted in the earth!

It did not take two months from that day when I received her call at about 10pm; she said, "Pastor, God answers your prayers you know." I said to her, "Is He not my Father?" "Please share the testimony." She said to me that her former principal called her that night and said to her, "I don't know what you have done to me, just come to the office tomorrow morning and pick up your cheque and stop tormenting my life." I asked her if she ever contacted him again after I said she should not, and she swore to me that she never did. I told her to go to the office the next day and pick up her cheque, which she did. She told me the next day that as soon as she got there and rang the office bell, the secretary brought an envelope to her at the entrance and that she didn't even see or speak with the Principal. God fought for her because she trusted Him. **Acts 10:34** says that our God is no respecter of persons. He will stand in defence of whoever puts their trust in Him.

～

MAYDAY HOSPITAL IN CROYDON, LONDON

One morning, one of my in-laws, Mazi Sunny, called me and told me about his friend who was admitted in hospital and the doctors could not diagnose what was wrong with him. He said he wanted to ask me if he could give my number to his friend so I could pray for him. I said he could and that he should also give me his friend's number so I could call him. Anyway, his friend called me and narrated his problem. I prayed for him over the phone, but he insisted I should come to the hospital. I asked the Evangelism department treasurer at the time, Ms. Alvanis to accompany me. On our arrival at the hospital, we located the ward and went in to see the patient. If not that Mazi Sunny already told me that the patient was a male, I would have thought that I was at the wrong place. What we saw shocked us. Lying down on the hospital bed was a man whose stomach looked like a woman pregnant with twins. When I asked if he was actually the person we were there to see and he confirmed that he was the one, I couldn't believe my eyes. The wife was standing there weeping. I trusted God Almighty to show up and He did. I prayed for him, anointed him and asked the wife to trust the Lord with me.

In the UK, doctors don't recommend treatment unless they have ascertained what the problem is. As at the time we got to the hospital, nothing had been ascertained to be the cause of his swollen stomach so they could not administer any medication.

The only thing I was told was that he had just come back from Nigeria where he had gone to either buy or sell some piece of land and as soon as he got back to the UK, he started experiencing that discomfort, a very strange one at that. His stomach was swollen as if he was pregnant with twins. To God be the glory, he received his miraculous healing.

One day my wife and I went to visit Mazi Sunny and his beloved wife who were having a feast in their place. The moment we got into the house somewhere in South East London, a very handsome looking young man embraced me and said to me "Thank you very much Pastor."

The moment he disengaged himself from me, a woman who I later was told is his wife did the same in the full glare of all the visitors there. I greeted them too and we took our seats. After a while I went into the kitchen where Mazi Sunny and his wife were busy preparing food and drinks for the visitors. When I told them what happened in the sitting room, Mazi Sunny said to me, "Pastor Solution, that is that my friend you went to pray for at Mayday Hospital in Croydon.

I then came back into the sitting room to greet him and his wife properly and apologised to them for not recognising them earlier when they both embraced me. There is no limit to what our God can do. He is Sovereign. He is all powerful. What He does is not a one-off. He is just waiting for who will trust Him to operate through them. Will you release your faith?

$$\sim$$

THE TESTIMONIES OF MR. AUSTIN

TESTIMONY NUMBER 1

One certain evening my cousin who is a well- known Barrister in the UK, Mazi Godwin took me out to eat at a popular African Restaurant in North London called Coal City, which is one of the oldest restaurants in the area. Being a very popular person, he has friends all over the city. On our arrival at the restaurant, just as I had witnessed previously, almost everyone there knew him. For some people, he handled their immigration applications, for some, their conveyancing when they acquired properties, while for some he could have handled some civil or criminal matters. It was not unusual to see people offering him drinks and other things just to show appreciation. Notable among those friends we met that night was one of his friends, Austin. He was a very pleasant fellow though. Handsome and lively. If you didn't notice him for those qualities, you would by his size. He was a huge guy. We happened to join him on his table in the restaurant and we had a very good time. My cousin introduced us and I just liked him. Besides that, I as an Evangelist, just don't let any opportunity I have to invite anyone to Church pass me by. So, I gave him my complimentary card and invited him to Church. He asked me to remind him on the Saturday before Sunday which I did. For several months, I kept inviting him every week and because he is a very sweet fella, I noticed that he never thought that I was disturbing him. After all, he willingly gave me his contact. After several months of inviting him and he promising to come and never honoured his word, I stopped calling him.

One afternoon, after two long years since our first meeting, he called me out of the blue. The moment I saw his call, I knew that there was a problem he needed God Almighty to resolve. When I picked the call, he started by introducing himself, but I told him not to bother as I had his contact on my phone. The first thing he said to me was, "Pastor, I am dying o." When I enquired, he told me he came back from Nigeria three days before and that he was poisoned back home. He was not able to go upstairs to his room. His legs were swollen and his skin was literally bursting and dripping fluid.

When I tried to pray for him over the phone, he insisted I must come in person. I knew that I needed to go immediately. He sent me his address and postcode. I hurriedly left work and drove to his house. When I rang the door-bell his nephew opened the door for me and let me into the house. I saw Mr. Izu on the sofa where he had been from the moment he got home from the airport.

He narrated his ordeal to me and told me how he went to Nigeria for a land matter, either to buy or to sell, I cannot remember. However, the consequence of it was the swelling feet the moment he got to his house in London. As you are looking at the swollen feet you could see the skin blistering and fluid coming out from the skin. I prayed a very simple prayer and used the anointing oil I always have with me, to anoint his feet and left. He also asked me if that was all, and I told him that the Lord would do what He alone can do; heal him.

The next day, at about 10am, I got his call and the first thing he said to me was, "Pastor Solution, where is your church?" I said to him that the church was still where it was since the two years we first met through my cousin and I had been inviting him. He told me that at about 4am on the same day after I visited to pray for him, he went upstairs to ease himself, flushed the toilet and his nephew came out from his room and asked him, "Uncle, what happened?" He said to his nephew, "You are asking me what happened in my own house?"

The nephew then said to him, "Uncle, since three days you came back from Nigeria this is the first time you would come up stairs to use the toilet. I have been the one bringing you a container downstairs to ease yourself." It was then that he looked at his feet and realised what the Lord had done. He said he would have called me at that hour but thought it was still too early. He came to the Church on Sunday and became a member of the Evangelism team of the Church.

TESTIMONY NUMBER 2

One day, after his mother-in-law's death and burial, he called to tell me that his little daughter was afraid to close her eyes because she was seeing her grandma each time she tried to sleep. I think she must have been about five years old at the time. I told him I was coming straight-away to his house. On arrival, I spoke and stood on God's word in **Psalm 127:2**, which says that God is the One who gives sleep to His beloved. I was still speaking when the little girl fell asleep in his father's arms. I did not make her fall asleep because I did not even touch her. I only stood on God's infallible word.

TESTIMONY NUMBER 3

I got yet another call, this time, they were hearing some strange noises in the house and everyone was afraid. He said they would be in the house and some strange things would be occurring. For instance, they would hear the toilet being flushed by some strange power, or some strange hands would open pots in the kitchen even though all the family members were in their respective rooms upstairs.

I went to the house and prayed and made declarations based on God's promises in **Job 22:28**, which says that I shall decree a thing and it shall be established. I commanded the strange powers to become paralysed forever in the name of Jesus Christ, the name above every other name, at the mention of which every other name must bow.

A few days later, he brought his whole family to the Church and after the service took them to the Associate Pastor's office to share the testimony. He said to the associate Pastor that he was quite surprised how the noises ceased immediately after I prayed. The associate Pastor then was Dr. Femi Idowu of blessed memory. He said to Mr. Austin, "Why are you surprised that the strange occurrences ceased? Don't you know who Pastor Solution represents?" He represents the Master, Jesus, the Christ, who will do exactly the same thing with whoever would make himself available, because He is no respecter of persons **[Acts 10:34]**.

AUNTIE GRACE'S TESTIMONY

In 2006, an auntie of mine, now late, had lost her husband. She would call me every morning at about 6am to pray for her and I would pray for her, even though at that same time I too was passing through some very serious time. I remember there were days I would hope she would not remember to call me because of the situation I was facing in my own life at the time. There were nights I couldn't sleep and hoped she would not call, but she never missed calling me for prayers. I could not tell her that I too was going through some tough times.

She would call me and the first thing she would say was, "It is me, Grace," to which I would respond, "Auntie, I know it is you." On this particular day, after praying for her, she said to me, "Solution, I am hearing noises inside my late husband's room; please can you come and open the room and pray so the noise would stop?" I told her I would come. I drove to her place and she gave me the keys to her late husband's room which had not been opened since his demise.

When I opened the door and went into the room, I felt a strange presence in there. As I prayed in that room, I felt goose pimples on my body. I prayed and decreed and commanded every strange presence to get out of the place. When I was done, I told the auntie that she would sleep peacefully in her home. She slept very peacefully in the house for several years until she left the house.

Indeed, if you release your faith, God will move for you.

MY YOUNGER BROTHER'S TESTIMONIES

Sometime around 2005, I was asleep when my phone rang and it was my younger brother, Franco calling from Lagos. When I answered, he said to me that they had been in hospital for two days because his wife was in labour and the baby wasn't coming out. I asked him to drop the phone so I could call him back. As I picked up my mobile phone to call him I discovered that I didn't have any money on the card to call Nigeria, so I decided to call him back on my landline, which I would normally not do due to the high charges. I had barely started praying and decreeing that every spirit of delay must lose their grip so she could deliver the baby, when I heard him shout, "Dede, omuola, Dede, Omuola." Which means "Dede she has delivered." (My younger ones address me as Dede), which is a sign of respect for an elder in my culture. The very same thing happened again during the delivery of their second child.

One of my cousins in London also had a similar experience. This time, the wife had been in labour for about four days. I asked him which hospital and he told me it was somewhere in Walthamstow, Whips Cross Hospital precisely. I went there, saw the wife, prayed with her and left. By the time I arrived home I got the good news that she had been delivered of a bouncing baby girl.

The thing is that once you put your faith to work the first time and get results, your faith becomes even stronger for the future. David understood this principle! That is why he was able to convince King Saul to allow him fight Goliath who had been terrorising Israel and made everyone's heart melt in the process. This is the account in **1 Samuel 17:34-37:**

> *"And Saul said to David, "You are not able to go against this Philistine to fight with him; for you are a youth, and he a man of war from his youth." But David said to Saul, "Your servant used to keep his father's sheep, and when a lion or a bear came and took a lamb out of the flock, and I went out after him, and smote him, and delivered it out of his mouth: and when he arose against me, I caught him by his beard, and smote him, and slew him. Your servant has killed both lion and bear; and this uncircumcised Philistine will be like one of them, seeing he has defied the armies of the living God. Moreover, David said, "The LORD, who delivered me from the paw of the lion and from the paw of the bear, He will deliver me from the hand of this Philistine." And Saul said to David, "Go, and the LORD be with you!"*

As you exercise your faith which is what overcomes for you, and God looks at that faith and overcomes for you, you will continually release faith for future challenges knowing that the same God who saw you through the last time will never abandon you. And as you continue to put your trust in Him, giving Him credit for all the previous victories, He will continue to perform the 'impossible' in your life. Then it becomes a pattern; an endless cycle and you will never stop living a life filled with testimonies. Hallelujah!

God works with our faith. In **Mark 9:23**, Jesus said,

> *"If only you can believe, ALL things are possible to him that believes."*

Why don't you dare to believe?

To let you know that God is indeed not a respecter of persons and does show up for whoever chooses to trust Him, I will talk briefly about a few people I know personally who chose to release their faith and the Lord did the rest.

CALABAR HALL, SURULERE, LAGOS

Through my cousin, Dr. Sam Chidozie Aka, who has now gone to be with the Lord Jesus, I was invited to preach at the Goshen Convention at the headquarters of Mountain Of Fire and Miracle Ministries in Lagos, Nigeria, in the year. During this engagement, the Lord connected me to several servants of God, among whom is Pastor Emmanuel Ejiogu, who runs a Prayer Ministry in Calabar Hall somewhere in Surulere, Lagos.

He invited me to preach at that fellowship. We agreed on a date after I would have travelled to different places in Nigeria, including my hometown to see my mum and a few other relatives. When I returned to Lagos on a Tuesday and the meeting was to be on a Thursday morning, I began to feel a strange pain in my right arm. It was a very painful and excruciating pain, such that it was very difficult to use the hand nor do anything else. After over twenty-four hours of nursing this pain that wouldn't abate despite all the medications, I managed to send a text message to the Pastor, informing him that I could not come for the programme that was to start at 6am that Thursday morning; this was only a few hours away, hoping he would reply with a text message too.

To my surprise, he called me immediately after he read my text message at about 4am, and said, "Pastor you cannot cancel, because I have already announced that you are coming and everyone is already eager to hear what the Lord will speak and do through you". At that point I had no option than to go to Surulere from my cousin's place at Victoria Island where I lodged. I did not even bother to take a bath before I left home, driving with one hand until I arrived at the place.

The moment I arrived, I asked him and some of his ministers to pray for me. I was still feeling that serious pain when I was invited to the pulpit to minister. A voice said to me, "You cannot even raise your right hand due to this pain, and you think people will believe what you preach about God having the power to do all things?" I rebuked that voice the same way I heard my mentor, Kenneth Copeland, say he silenced that voice when he was faced with a similar situation; he had gone to preach somewhere in America and suddenly began to experience excruciating pain on one leg that made him visibly limp. The moment I scolded that liar, Satan, and walked to the pulpit to receive the microphone, that pain ceased, and I ministered as though I never felt any pain before I got to that meeting. I preached and laid hands-on people and the Lord performed some great miracles on that day.

The devil's trick is to play a fast one on believers so he can erode their faith in God. Imagine that the reason I didn't want to appear at the event was so that people wouldn't say, "How can this man in such gruesome pain make us believe that God still heals?" However, the moment I released my faith, I got my instant healing and allowed the Lord to minister through me. By the time I finished, the congregation asked that I be brought back again to minister. By the grace of God, that place has become home for me and I have preached there up to five or six times.

Just imagine what difference my not appearing the first time would have made! Apostle Paul said, in **2 Corinthians 2:11 [MSG]**,

"After all, we don't want to unwittingly give Satan an opening for yet more mischief—we're not oblivious to his sly ways!"

~

REV. FEMI OMISADE

One of our pastors, Rev. Ade Omotunde was having a surprise birthday party organised by his wife, Rev. Fola, and the venue was packed when it was discovered that the equipment which had been functioning properly suddenly stopped working. Nothing all the experienced technicians did would make the instruments function. When all failed, one of our Pastors, the DGO at the time, Rev. Omisade, got up and laid hands on the equipment, muttered a few words and the equipment obeyed.

A few years later at the wife Rev. Fola Omotunde's birthday party in another venue, something similar occurred. Remembering what my DGO at the time did a few years prior, I also went to mutter some silent words over the equipment, laid my hands on the instruments and said in the name of Jesus Christ start functioning. They started functioning instantly to the glory of God. Glory to Jesus. Faith indeed works!! After all, just as I said earlier, it is written in the Book of **Psalm 18:44-45**,

"When they hear of Me they shall obey Me, and the strangers will submit themselves and come out from their hiding places."

Jesus has all the powers (**Matthew 28:18**), and Jesus and His Word are one. (Revelations 19:13 says that His name is the Word of God). Whatever Jesus can do, His Word will also do.

THE TESTIMONY OF A WOMAN IN MY CHURCH

Several years ago, after the Lord brought me to New Covenant Church, Edmonton in London, I was leading a House Fellowship where I was privileged to hear an incredible testimony from one of our Church members, a very wonderful lady and a true believer. She narrated to me how when she was pregnant with her first child, she went for a scan. The result of the scan said that the child in her womb was a boy and had down syndrome. That was the greatest blow she ever received in her entire life. She was advised to give her consent so the pregnancy could be aborted in order to save her from an untold and needless trouble of seeing the pregnancy to the end. She told the doctors that she would have to get home and discuss with her husband before she could decide the next line of action. When she got home and broke the sad news to the young man, he too was devastated but could only say to her, "Darling, since you are the one carrying the pregnancy, whatever you decide is okay by me."

Some other family members and friends advised her to terminate the pregnancy as she was too young to "condemn" herself to a life of looking after a child with disability, and that she would still get pregnant thereafter. She was still going through this whole confusion of what to do, when suddenly Satan made the mistake of reminding her of what she did as a very young girl when she didn't know Jesus. A voice said to her, "This is the repercussion of the sin you committed when you were in college." That was when she realised that she needed to trust God and put the devil, the liar, in his deserved place with the Word of God.

She remembered the Bible says in **2 Corinthians 5:17** that if any man be in Christ, he is a new creation; old things are passed away and behold all things have become new. She remembered that the Lord said to her in **Isaiah 43:18-19**,

"Do not remember the former things, behold I will do a new thing."

She reminded the Lord of His promises in **Isaiah 1:18** which says,

"Come back and let us reason together, though your sins be like scarlet, they shall become as white as snow, and though they be like crimson, they shall become as wool."

She remembered the Word of God in **Isaiah 43:25**,

"I am He, who for my namesake I forgive your iniquities, and your sins will I remember no more."

She reminded herself that it is written in **Psalm 103:3**, that God forgives all our iniquities and heals all our diseases. She remembered **John 3:17**,

"For God did not send His Son into the world to condemn the world, but that the world through Him might be saved."

She chose to trust God. She did not stop reminding God of all His promises up till the day she delivered her baby.

She gave birth to a bouncing baby girl, a very beautiful and healthy girl for that matter as against a boy with down syndrome. The same doctors could not believe what they saw and they unanimously called it a miracle, and some of them who witnessed this miracle joined her to believe in her God. Today, that daughter has graduated from the university as a doctor herself and is happily married with her own son. Just imagine what would have been if my church member hadn't chosen to trust God! Perhaps she would have ended up not having any child at all. She has three beautiful children who all have graduated from university. It pays to trust God. In **John 2:5**, Mary said, *"Whatever He says to you, do it."* It pays to believe God and His Word. That is FAITH.

DEAD PASTOR RAISED FROM THE DEAD DUE TO THE WIFE'S STUBBORN FAITH

One of the people I believe demonstrated what I can call 'stubborn faith' was the wife of one Pastor, Daniel Ekechukwu in Nigeria who was involved in a fatal road accident. He was taken to a hospital at Owerri in the present Imo State where unfortunately he lost the battle as the doctors could not save him despite all their efforts. The wife vehemently refused that her husband would be buried, but rather insisted that she be allowed to take his body to Onitsha in Anambra State where the late Reinhard Bonke was having a programme, her reason being that she had read what **Hebrews 11:35** said,

"Women received back their dead, raised to life again."

She kept on saying to God that she too is a woman and that she trusted Him to raise her husband from the dead. After much pressure the family allowed her to take the corpse to the crusade venue where the preacher, Bonnke was having the programme. On arrival she explained herself to the security men who then contacted the host, the Senior Pastor of the Church who subsequently allowed her to be taken to the basement of the church where some people were asked to go pray with her.

Let's see how Reinhard Bonnke put it when interviewed by Pat Robertson of CBN.

Below are the excerpts of the interview:

Robertson: I want you to tell me about the testimonies like the man coming back to life in one of the meetings. He was hit by a car. I understand he was stiff and rigor mortis had set in. I don't know if they had embalmed him or not.

Bonnke: They did.

Robertson: He had been embalmed?

Bonnke: He was embalmed, but not the way it is done in America with the removal of organs. They injected chemicals into the body to slow down decay, since there was no refrigeration.

Robertson: So what happened?

Bonnke: His wife was one with a promise from God that women have received back the dead by resurrection. She said, "My husband will come back, and I have heard Reinhard Bonnke is in Onitsha this Sunday. I will bring him there. She brought him there. I was preaching and I knew nothing about it. Suddenly the man started to breathe. His story is awesome and what he was shown while he was in eternity.

Robertson: Tell me, what did he see?

Bonnke: An angel took him to show him Paradise. He showed him the mansions that are waiting for the saints. And showed him hell. He saw the people in hell. He said one shouted to him, "I was a Pastor and I stole money. Help me return the money." He said it was so frightening to him that the angel turned to him and said, "The prayer of the rich man in Luke 16 will now be fulfilled, and you will be sent back to earth as a last warning to this generation."

Robertson: For those who are not aware of that, in Luke 16 the rich man lifted up his eyes in torment and said, "I have a number of brothers. Let me go back and warn them." Father Abraham said, "No, they have Moses and the prophets. If they won't believe them, they will not believe the one who rose from the dead. Now, he says that on the last day, he's going to be the one? He has come back?

Bonnke: He has come back. People who see this video *(Raised from the Dead)* are getting saved by the thousands. I hear reports from across the world. It is such a powerful tool of evangelism and we are absolutely delighted. I wish I could have produced Pastor Daniel here today.

Robertson: We tried to get him through customs, but it is so tough in America to get a visa in this country. We couldn't get him in. You say he saw hell. Were there fires? Torment?

Bonnke: He said he saw no fire but he said he saw these people cannibalising themselves. Every time they had done it, the flesh seemed to jump back to the same places and then the torment started again. He said it was so horrible. He came back and said, "Heaven is real. Hell is real. Become serious with God. You need to be saved by the blood of Jesus Christ and live a holy life."

Robertson: I want to stop right now, ladies and gentlemen, and ask, where are you in the Lord? Are you playing games with God? Where are you with God? Reinhard, give this audience a word about how they can come to Jesus. We will talk more about these crusades, but there are people right now who need to be spared from hell.

Bonnke: It is true. I would say it this way. We have to say "yes" to Jesus. Many have done that, but when saying "yes" to Jesus, we must say at the same time "no" to sin.

Otherwise, that "yes" to Jesus is invalid. We cannot walk in two directions at the same time. If we do, we fool ourselves. That would be very terrible, like that Pastor that was witnessed there. Say "yes" to Jesus from the bottom of your heart and turnaround from unrighteousness. Repent of your sins and receive forgiveness by the blood of Jesus Christ. Then walk the path of righteousness. Whosoever calls upon the name of the Lord shall be saved. Let's pray together right now. Pray, *"Dear Lord Jesus, I say "yes" to you and "no" to sin. Forgive me of my sins. Wash me with your precious blood. Come into my heart, Lord Jesus. In Jesus name, Amen."*

Robertson: Amen. Those who prayed with Reinhard call us at 1-800-759-0700 and we will send you a free booklet called "A New Beginning." We want you to be established in the Lord. And whether you want literature or not just call us and say that you prayed. Hell is real. Hell is real. The Bible talks about it and Jesus talks about it. What that man was saying, Reinhard, was that it wasn't so much the literal flames, but the flames of missed opportunity and the anguish of conscience. And these people are gnawing on their own flesh because they hate what they have done so much they are trying to destroy themselves but can't?

Bonnke: All accused themselves. They didn't blame anyone else. He said that they didn't see the angel next to him. They only saw him and were calling for help. The angel turned around and said that Daniel would be connected to me and that through me this testimony would be spread across the whole world. Suddenly Daniel gasped for air in the church. He was there in the basement while I was preaching upstairs, "In the name of Jesus!" It is awesome. I mean that story has covered Nigeria, Africa, and the world.

Robertson: I am sure this man was not learned in the Bible, but the Apostle Paul says your own conscience will either excuse or accuse you on the day of Jesus Christ. So their own conscience was their accuser. They were accusing themselves?

Bonnke: Yes. Yes they do.

Robertson: They weren't covering up anymore. A Pastor had been stealing money. He was essentially a fraud and a hypocrite and he was in hell crying out for help?

Bonnke: Yes.

Robertson: But there is no help. Once they are there, they are there. It is permanent.

Bonnke: That is so. You know, you mentioned about the missed opportunity.

Robertson: Oh, dear!

Bonnke: They keep on missing it because there is no opportunity.

Robertson: What did he see in heaven?

Bonnke: He saw the saints worshipping. He said it was so wonderful he wanted to enter that place. My question to him was "Did you see Jesus?" He said there was a white, bright light and all of those saints were worshipping and looking in that direction. He said, "I shaded my eyes, but my eyes could not penetrate it." Then he was taken to the mansions. He tried to describe the beauty of those mansions. He said, "Like, like, like."

Robertson: He didn't have the words.

Bonnke: He said he was told the mansions are ready but the saints are not.

Robertson: Oh, my! Did Jesus or anyone give him a warning for the church? Did he come back and say something to those who are supposed to be living for the Lord?

Bonnke: He had another fearful experience. I didn't know this Pastor Daniel at all. He said that the angel said to him, "If God had not decided to send you back to earth, you would join the people in hell." He was shaking.

Robertson: But this guy is a Pastor. What was it?

Bonnke: He was a man who didn't live right.

Robertson: So he was a fraud.

Bonnke: He was not living right. He now lives right.

Robertson: But if he hadn't had that experience, he would have joined those in hell.?

Bonnke: That is what he was told.

Robertson: Oh, my goodness! That, Reinhard, is a much tougher standard than we are used to. We are thinking here in America of easy grace and I am a good guy.

Bonnke: My own television team that made that video said they couldn't sleep for three nights and everybody brought their lives up to standard, the standard of the Word of God. It brought a lot of heart searching.

Robertson: Did this man have a chance to speak his testimony to that multitude that came to hear you?

Bonnke: He was at my crusade. It was fantastic. I had him in Vienna. At the same time, while I had my meetings there, there was an esoteric convention there. When they heard that someone had come back from the dead, they loved to hear the voices from the dead, and they said, "Can you not address us?" He went to speak to them, preached, and made an altar call and 50 witches got saved.

Robertson: This is incredible. Do you have a video?

Bonnke: It is right here [Raised from the Dead]. So many pray for their loved one. This is a step further. This really is a call to salvation that is very urgent.

Robertson: I am inspired to have you with us.

Reinhard Bonnke ended by saying that God did not raise the dead because he was preaching (since he didn't even know what was happening at the basement of the church while he preached upstairs), but that God raised him because of the STUBBORN FAITH of the wife.

Brethren, if our faith is stubborn and radical, there is nothing God Almighty cannot do. I truly wish that some of these testimonies I have shared will help encourage you and help you grow your faith.

CHAPTER 8
GROW YOUR FAITH

We have been told in several instances in this book that we all have been given a measure of faith. How do we know this? The simple answer is through the Word of God. It therefore follows that the primary or the main source of faith is the Word of God. This is made very clear in **Romans 10:17**. I will quote that very verse from at least four different versions of the Bible (AMP; MSG; NLT and NKJV).

- *"So faith comes by hearing [what is told], and what is heard comes by the preaching [of the message that came from the lips] of Christ (the Messiah Himself)."* **[AMP]**
- *"The point is, before you trust, you have to listen. But unless Christ's Word is preached, there is nothing to listen to."* **[MSG]**
- *"Yet faith comes from listening to the message of good news-the Good News about Christ."* **[NLT]**
- *"So then faith comes by hearing, and hearing by the word of God."* **[NKJV]**

The Bible tells us that in the beginning was the word, the word was with God and the word was God. Therefore, when we are told that God gives to each one a measure of faith, [Romans 12:3], and that faith comes through the word, there is nothing confusing about that.

HOW CAN ONE GROW THEIR FAITH?

The Apostle Paul wrote to the Church in Thessalonica to encourage them to grow in their faith. "We ought and indeed are obligated [as those in debt] to give thanks always to God for you, brethren, as is fitting, because your FAITH IS GROWING EXCEEDINGLY and the love of every one of you each toward the others is increasing and abounds."

One of the signs that your faith is growing is that you will start loving exactly like God loves.

You can grow your faith in the following ways:

1. READ, STUDY AND MEDITATE ON THE WORD OF GOD

In the words of Danny Anderson, The Bible is a book written with the intention to produce faith in you. **John 20:31** says,

> *"But these are written that you may believe that Jesus is the Messiah, the Son of God, and that by believing you may have life in His name."*

When you read the Scriptures, you are taking in the truth about what God is like and what He has done. It is a testimony to His character and work in this world. If you want to grow your faith you must have a regular diet of the Word of God by reading the Bible.

2. PUT THE WORD INTO PRACTICE

The Bible says we should be doers of the Word and not just hearers. Jesus puts it this way,

> *"Therefore everyone who hears these words of mine and puts them into practice is like a wise man who built his house on the rock. The rain came down, the storm rose, and the winds blew and beat against that house; yet it did not fall, because it had its foundation on the rock."*
> **[Matthew 7:24-25]**

When you put the Words of God in practice, you will see your life slowly start to change, and your faith will grow in the process. I always make this illustration whenever I tell people how to put their faith in motion. If you have a car with power steering, as long as the car is parked on one spot, turning the steering will prove difficult, but the moment you move the car a little bit you will find that the steering becomes easier to manipulate. It is not because the car didn't have power steering all along. It is just that the vehicle was on one spot. You cannot discover how effective your faith is until you put it to work.

3. SURROUND YOURSELF WITH PEOPLE OF FAITH

It does matter the type of people you surround yourself with. **Deuteronomy 20:8** says,

> *"The officers will then continue, "And is there a man here who is wavering in resolve and afraid? Let him go home right now so that he doesn't infect his fellows with his timidity and cowardly spirit."*
> **[MSG]**

Joshua 14:8 says,

"My companions who went with me discouraged the people, but I stuck to my guns, totally with GOD my God. [MSG]

Someone said with regards to relationships; "Show me your friends and I will show you your future." According to Jim Rohn, "You are the average of the five people you spend the most time with. Whether we know it or not, we have the tendency to be influenced by the people we spend time with. The company we keep has the tendency to either help strengthen our faith or erode it.

If you are in doubt, see what **Numbers 13:31-33** has to say,

"But the others said, "We can't attack those people; they're way stronger than we are." They spread scary rumours against the people of Israel. They said, "We scouted out the land from one end to the other-it's a land that swallows people whole. Everybody we saw was huge. Why, we even saw the Nephilim giants (the Anak giants come from the Nephilim). Alongside them we felt like grasshoppers. And they looked down on us as if we were grasshoppers." [MSG]

Numbers 14:1-3 –

"Then all the people began weeping aloud, and they cried all night. Their voices rose in a great chorus of complaints against Moses and Aaron. "We wish we had died in Egypt, or even here in the wilderness!" they wailed. "Why is the Lord taking us to this country only to have us die in battle? Our wives and little ones will be carried off as slaves! Let's get out of here and return to Egypt!"

From the above three scriptures, it is obvious that the company one keeps determines whether their faith will work or fail. See how the evil report derailed the entire destiny of the Israelites. No wonder **Proverbs 13:20** says,

If you walk with the wise you will become wise, but if fools are your companions, then destruction is imminent."

This view is supported in **1 Corinthians 15:33**. It says that *"evil communication will surely destroy good manners."* This same principle applies when it comes to your faith.

Look around you and see the people you spend your time with. Are they people of faith? If their faith is stronger than yours then it will rub off on you and your faith will grow, but if the reverse is the case, then your faith will not grow. Make it a habit to mingle with people who believe in God and speak His word, knowing that He is always in control. A clear demonstration of this truth is found in **2 Kings 3:14**. Some kings were in trouble and needed help so they went to meet God's servant, Prophet Elisha. He said to them that he would listen to them simply because they were in the company of Jehoshaphat for whom he had regard.

"And Elisha said, As the Lord of hosts lives, before Whom I stand, surely, were it not that I respect the presence of Jehoshaphat king of Judah, I would neither look at you nor see you [King Joram]"

So, it is time to conduct an internal audit! I would urge you to look around you and ensure that you are in the right company of people.

4. READ GREAT BOOKS OF PEOPLE WHOSE FAITH WILL INSPIRE AND CHALLENGE YOURS.

Apart from the Bible, you can read great books of men that can build your faith. Authors like C. S. Lewis, Brennan Manning, John Piper, Kenneth Hagin, Oral Roberts, Kenneth Copeland, Bishop Oyedepo, Rev. Dr. Paul Jinadu, and my books detailing my experiences with drugs, prison cycle, depression and its inherent suicide attempts and how the Lord delivered me through His grace, can build your faith. Paul said to Timothy,

> *"When you come, be sure to bring the coat I left with Carpus at Troas. Also bring my books, and especially my papers."*

This shows that in addition to the Scriptures, Paul also valued the writings of other mentors of faith.

5. TRUST GOD IN THE PAIN

Just believe that if He allows you into it, He will also see you through it.

God said to Peter in **Luke 22:31-32,**

> *"Simon, Simon! Indeed, Satan has asked for you, that he may sift you as wheat. But I have prayed for you, that your FAITH should not fail; and when you have returned to Me, strengthen your brethren."*

This shows that before you encounter any situation, the Lord who knows the end from the beginning already knows about it. What is important to know is that so long as the enemy cannot weaken your faith, he cannot defeat you. He knows too well that it is your faith that will overcome him **[1 John 5:4].** The three Hebrew boys were determined not to bow to the devil even if they were thrown into the fiery furnace, and their resolve made God show up for them. The fiery furnace became an air-conditioned room because Jesus showed up in their trial as a result of their faith in the Lord.

Let us look at **Daniel 3:8-30 [AMP],**

> *"At that time certain Chaldeans came forward and brought [malicious] accusations against the Jews. They said to King Nebuchadnezzar,*

"O king, live forever! You, O king, have made a decree that everyone who hears the sound of the horn, pipe, lyre, trigon, harp, dulcimer, bagpipe, and all kinds of music is to fall down and worship the golden image. Whoever does not fall down and worship shall be thrown into the midst of a furnace of blazing fire. There are certain Jews whom you have appointed over the administration of the province of Babylon, namely Shadrach, Meshach, and Abed-nego. These men, O king, pay no attention to you; they do not serve your gods or worship the golden image which you have set up."

Then Nebuchadnezzar in a furious rage gave a command to bring Shadrach, Meshach, and Abed-nego; and these men were brought before the king. Nebuchadnezzar said to them, "Is it true, Shadrach, Meshach, and Abed-nego, that you do not serve my gods or worship the golden image which I have set up? Now if you are ready, when you hear the sound of the horn, pipe, lyre, trigon, harp, dulcimer, and all kinds of music, to fall down and worship the image which I have made, very good. But if you do not worship, you shall be thrown at once into the midst of a furnace of blazing fire; and what god is there who can rescue you out of my hands?"

Shadrach, Meshach, and Abed-nego answered the king, "O king Nebuchadnezzar, we do not need to answer you on this point. If it be so, our God whom we serve is able to rescue us from the furnace of blazing fire, and He will rescue us from your hand, O king. But even if He does not, let it be known to you, O king, that we are not going to serve your gods or worship the golden image that you have set up!"

Then Nebuchadnezzar was filled with fury, and his facial expression changed toward Shadrach, Meshach, and Abed-nego. Then he gave a command that the furnace was to be heated seven [a]times hotter than usual. He commanded certain strong men in his army to tie up Shadrach, Meshach, and Abed-nego and to throw them into the furnace of blazing fire. Then these [three] men were tied up in their trousers, their coats, their turbans, and their other clothes, and were thrown into the midst of the furnace of blazing fire. Because the king's command was urgent and the furnace was extremely hot, the flame of the fire killed the men who carried up Shadrach, Meshach, and Abed-nego. But these three men, Shadrach, Meshach, and Abed-nego, fell into the midst of the furnace of blazing fire still tied up.

Then Nebuchadnezzar the king [looked and] was astounded, and he jumped up and said to his counsellors, "Did we not throw three men who were tied up into the midst of the fire?" They replied to the king, "Certainly, O king." He answered, "Look! I see four men untied, walking around in the midst of the fire, and they are not hurt! And the appearance of the fourth is like [b]a son of the gods!" Then Nebuchadnezzar approached the door of the blazing furnace and said, "Shadrach, Meshach, and Abed-nego, servants of the Most High God, come out [of there]! Come here!" Then Shadrach, Meshach, and Abed-nego came out of the midst of the fire. The satraps, the prefects, the governors and the king's counsellors gathered around them and saw that in regard to these men the fire had no effect on their bodies—their hair was not singed, their clothes were not scorched or damaged, even the smell of smoke was not on them.

Nebuchadnezzar responded and said, "Blessed be the God of Shadrach, Meshach, and Abed-nego, who has sent His angel and rescued His servants who believed in, trusted in, and relied on Him! They violated the king's command and surrendered their bodies rather than serve or worship any god except their own God. Therefore I make a decree that any people, nation, or language that speaks anything offensive against the God of Shadrach, Meshach, and Abed-nego shall be cut into pieces and their houses be made a heap of rubbish, for there is no other god who is able to save in this way!"

Then the king caused Shadrach, Meshach, and Abed-nego to prosper in the province of Babylon."

It is evident that the stubborn faith in their God made the difference. Ours is not just a God of yesterday. He is also the God of now and the future. Have you been accused unjustly and it is looking as though there is no way out for you? Jesus is not just the Way Maker; He is THE WAY. Put your trust in Him and He will see you through any challenges of life. It is written that Whosoever puts his trust in Him shall NOT be ashamed **[Romans 10:11].**

Moreover, our stubborn faith can be contagious to the point that people will drop their idols and start worshipping the only true God.

6. PRAY IN TONGUES

Jude 1:20 [MSG]:

> *But you, dear friends, carefully build yourselves up in this most holy faith by praying in the Holy Spirit.*

Why should our faith remain stagnant when we can make it grow? The choice is ours and it is indeed our responsibility to grow our faith.

CHAPTER 9
HINDRANCES TO FAITH OPERATION

There are things that can prevent or hinder our faith from functioning. I would like to discuss some of the factors that could hinder faith operation and I dare say that this list is not exhaustive by any means. I will also give tips on how to overcome these hindrances.

1. FEAR

Someone described FEAR as False Evidence Appearing Real. Often, the way one looks at things may give them the identity they do not really merit. Fear is one great enemy that can hinder faith from winning for anyone. A typical example is the story of the twelve spies Moses had sent to the land they were to go and occupy.

THE TWELVE SPIES – NUMBERS 13:25-33 [NLT]

After exploring the land for forty days, the men returned to Moses, Aaron, and the people of Israel at Kadesh in the Wilderness of Paran. They reported to the whole community what they had seen and showed them the fruit they had taken from the land. This was their report to

Moses: "We arrived in the land you sent us to see, and it is indeed a magnificent country-a land flowing with milk and honey. Here is some of its fruit as proof. But the people living there are powerful, and their cities and towns are fortified and very large. We also saw the descendants of Anak who are living there! The Amalekites live in the Negev, and the Hittites, Jebusites, and the Amorites live in the hill country. The Canaanites live along the coast of the Mediterranean Sea and along the Jordan Valley." But Caleb tried to encourage the people as they stood before Moses. "Let's go at once to take the land," he said. "We can certainly conquer it!" But the other men who had explored the land with him answered, "We can't go up against them! They are stronger than we are!" So they spread discouraging reports about the land among the Israelites: "The land we explored will swallow up anyone who goes to live there. All the people we saw were huge. We even saw giants there, the descendants of Anak. We felt like grasshoppers next to them, and that's what we looked like to them!"

In fact, the **NKJV** puts verse 33 this way:

There we saw giants (the descendants of Anak came from the giants); and we were like grasshoppers in our own sight, and so we were in their sight."

Now, I have no problem if in their own sight they looked like grasshoppers to the giants. My problem is with their own assertion and admission that they also looked like grasshoppers in the sight of those giants. How could they have said such a thing when they never entered the eyes of those giants. They just assumed that. It is foolish to assume such a thing. Anonymous says, ASSUME makes ASS U and ME.

Rather than assume, let us search the Scriptures to hear what God has to say. In **Isaiah 7:4**, the Lord says, whenever you face challenges and issues of life, do these FOUR things:

(a) Take heed.
(b) Be Quiet.
(c) Do not FEAR.
(d) Do not be fainthearted.

To take heed means to listen to the next instruction and know the next line of action.

To be quiet will enable you to hear what the instructions are.

Do not fear means FEAR and FAITH cannot be a good mixture.

Do not be faint hearted despite all, just keep waiting on the Lord. (**Isaiah 6:4** says there is a reward in waiting on God despite the challenge).

After all, God's Word says in the Book of **Jeremiah 29:10-11 [MSG],**

> This is GOD's Word on the subject: "As soon as Babylon's seventy years are up and not a day before, I'll show up and take care of you as I promised and bring you back home. I know what I'm doing. I have it all planned out-plans to take care of you, not abandon you, plans to give you the future you hope for.

This means as we wait for His intervention, we must not give up.

We cannot hurry Him. He is sovereign. **Hebrews 10: 36-39 [AMP]** says:

> For you have need of steadfast patience and endurance, so that you may perform and fully accomplish the will of God, and thus receive and carry away [and enjoy to the full] what is promised. For still a little

while (a very little while), and the Coming One will come and He will not delay. But the just shall live by faith [My righteous servant shall live by his conviction respecting man's relationship to God and divine things, and holy fervour born of faith and conjoined with it]; and if he draws back and shrinks in FEAR, my soul has no delight or pleasure in him. But our way is not that of those who draw back to eternal misery (perdition) and are destroyed, but we are of those who believe [who cleave to and trust in and rely on God through Jesus Christ, the Messiah] and by FAITH preserve the soul.

2. DOUBT/FOCUSING ON CHALLENGES

Doubt is another major hindrance to the operation of our faith. God tells us that his ways are higher than our ways and thus if faith is believing what God says, it becomes a struggle because the things he says seem impossible to us. If we choose to walk by our own understanding, then doubt creeps in and becomes a hindrance because it diffuses our faith.

Jesus said in the Book of **Mark 11: 23-24 [AMP]**:

Truly I tell you, whoever says to this mountain, be lifted up and thrown down into the sea! And does not DOUBT at all in his heart but believes that what he says will take place, it will be done for him. For this reason, I am telling you, whatever you ask for in prayer, believe (trust and be confident) that it is granted to you, and you will [get it].

An example of how doubt can deflate and derail one's faith can be found in the Book of **Matthew 14:22-32**. Peter would have been the only one who would have gone down in history as the man who walked on the water after Jesus Christ if not that he doubted albeit momentarily. Let's look at the story:

"Immediately after this, Jesus made His disciples get back into the boat and cross to the other side of the lake while He sent the people home. Afterward He went up into the hills by Himself to pray. Night fell while He was there alone. Meanwhile, the disciples were in trouble far away from land, for a strong wind had risen, and they were fighting heavy waves. And in the fourth watch of the night Jesus went unto them, walking on the sea. When the disciples saw Him, they screamed in terror, thinking He was a ghost. But Jesus spoke to them at once. "It's all right," He said, "I am here! Don't be afraid." Then Peter called to Him, "Lord, if it's really you, tell me to come to you by WALKING on the water." "All right, come," Jesus said. So Peter went over the side of the boat and WALKED on the water toward Jesus. But when he looked around at the high waves, he was terrified and began to sink. "Save me, Lord!" he shouted. Instantly, Jesus reached out His hand and grabbed him. "You don't have much FAITH," Jesus said. "Why did you DOUBT me?" And when they climbed back into the boat, the wind stopped".

We can observe from the above that had Peter not doubted Jesus's words, he would have walked on the water up to where Jesus was. The fact that he doubted meant that the water that had become a kind of solid ground for him to walk on, dissolved immediately. Any iota of doubt is enough to dissolve any person's faith. We must never mix doubt with faith. It is like mixing water and fuel. There is no way the engine will perform at its full capacity if petrol is mixed with water.

The Holy Book in **Hebrews 4:1-3 [AMP]** further illustrates this:

"Therefore, while the promise of entering His rest still holds and is offered [today], let us be AFRAID [to DISTRUST it], lest any of you should think he has come too late and has come short of [reaching it]. For unto us was the gospel preached, as well as unto them: but the word preached did not profit them, not being mixed with FAITH in them

that heard it. For we who have believed (adhered to and trusted in and relied on God) do enter that rest, in accordance with His declaration that those [who did NOT believe] should not enter when He said, as I swore in My wrath, they shall not enter My rest; and this He said although [His] works had been completed and prepared [and waiting for all who would believe] from the foundation of the world."

The apostle James uses a specific example (praying for wisdom) to show that wavering doubt can remain a major hurdle to faith if it is not addressed:

"If any of you lacks wisdom, let him ask of God ... But let him ask in faith, with no doubting, for he who doubts is like a wave of the sea driven and tossed by the wind. For let not that man suppose that he will receive anything from the Lord; he is a double-minded man, unstable in all his ways" **[James 1:5-8]**

Being "unstable" means unable to stand – as Peter was on the waves.

Overcoming this doubt or "double-mindedness" involves constantly being aware of God working in our lives so that we see the ongoing evidence that He is, indeed, working with us personally.

3. LACK OF LOVE

The importance of Love cannot be overemphasised. Have you ever wondered what faith and love have to do with one another? How are they connected? Let us examine this connection.

Galatians 5:4-6 NLT says:

"For if you are trying to make yourselves right with God by keeping the law, you have been cut off from Christ! You have fallen away from God's GRACE. But who will live by the Spirit eagerly wait to receive

everything promised to us who are right with God through FAITH. For, when we place our FAITH in Christ Jesus, it makes no difference to God whether we are circumcised or not circumcised. What is important is FAITH expressing itself in love."

The NKJV puts verse 6 as *FAITH working through LOVE.*

To quote Gloria Copeland in her write up *How are Faith and Love Connected?*

Faith works by love. It is energized by love. Faith is put into motion by love. Why is that, you may ask? Let's look at the teaching by Apostle Paul on love in 1 Corinthians 13. I want us to read verses 1-3 focusing on the faith-love connection.

"If I [can] speak in the tongues of men and [even] of angels but have not love...I am only a noisy gong or a clanging cymbal. And if I have prophetic powers...and if I have [sufficient] faith so that I can remove mountains but have not love (God's love in me) I am nothing (a useless nobody). Even if I dole out all that I have [to the poor in providing] food, and if I surrender my body to be burned...but have not love...I gain nothing" **[AMP]**

We have only one commandment! We are to walk in love, which covers a lot of ground. In fact, we see in this passage that our love walk is connected to everything we do in life as believers, including our faith. Paul makes it quite clear that faith without love is going nowhere.

Without love our FAITH is FAKE. Whoever claims to be in Christ and is harbouring wickedness, unforgiveness and bitterness is deceiving himself because God's GRACE cannot stay where those things operate. Never!

CeCe Winans in her song summarised the importance of love fuelling our faith. She said that without love there is no need to prophesy. Without love we are all wasting time because love is the strongest. She says that love is the key and the greatest gift.

The importance of love kickstarting our faith cannot be overemphasised. We don't do people any favours by loving them. It fires up our own faith so we can move mountains. Glory to God!

4. UNFORGIVENESS/BITTERNESS

Bitterness is poisonous. Unforgiveness is like drinking a glass of poison and expecting your enemy to fall and die. Anyone who walks in unforgiveness does evil to himself. Bitterness affects and destroys him rather than his enemy. There is no doubt that unforgiveness is a major hindrance to our faith.

Let's look at **Mark 11:22-26** in the NLT and AMP translations:

> *"Then Jesus said to the disciples, "Have faith in God." I assure you that you can say to this mountain, "May God lift you up and throw you into the sea," and your command will be obeyed. All that's required is that you REALLY BELIEVE and do not DOUBT in your heart. Listen to Me! You can pray for anything, and if you BELIEVE, you will have it. But when praying, first FORGIVE anyone you are holding a grudge against, so that your Father in heaven will forgive your sins, too." [NLT]*

> *"But if you do not forgive, neither will your Father in heaven forgive your failings and shortcomings." [AMP]*

Let's see **Hebrews 12:15** in three different versions to drive home this point.

Exercise foresight and be on the watch to look [after one another], to see that no one falls back from and fails to secure God's GRACE (His unmerited favour and spiritual blessing), in order that no root of resentment (rancour, bitterness, or hatred) shoots forth and causes trouble and bitter torment, and the many become contaminated and defiled by it. [**AMP**]

Make sure no one gets left out of God's generosity. Keep a sharp eye out for weeds of bitter discontent. A thistle or two gone to seed can ruin a whole garden in no time. [**MSG**]

Look after each other so that none of you will miss out on the special favour of God. Watch out that no bitter root of UNBELIEF rises among you, for whenever it springs up, many are corrupted by its poison. [**NLT**]

5. TRADITION/RELIGION

Jesus telling believers what can hinder their faith, says in **Mark 7:13 [AMP]**:

Thus, you are nullifying and making void and of no effect [the authority] of the Word of God through your TRADITION, which you [in turn] hand on. And many things of this kind you are doing.

Whoever is in Christ should know that he is now a member of a new family just as **2 Corinthians 5:17** makes it clear. A believer is no longer bound by their tradition but he is bound by how things are done in this new kingdom.

Ephesians 4:24-32 makes it even clearer what he who has exchanged families/tradition ought to do.

You MUST display a new nature because you are a new person, created in God's likeness-righteous, holy, and true. So put away all falsehood and "tell your neighbour the truth" because we belong to each other. And "don't sin by letting anger gain control over you. "Don't let the sun go down while you are still angry, for anger gives a MIGHTY foothold to the Devil. If you are a thief, stop stealing. Begin using your hands for honest work, and then give generously to others in need. Don't use foul or abusive language. Let EVERY-THING you say be good and helpful, so that your words will be an encouragement to those who hear them. And do not bring sorrow to God's Holy Spirit by the way you live. Remember, He is the One who has identified you as His own, guaranteeing that you will be saved on the day of redemption. Get rid of bitterness, rage, anger, harsh words, and slander, as well as all types of malicious behaviour. Instead, be kind to each other, tender-hearted, forgiving one another, just as God through Christ has forgiven you.

6. NEGLECTING THE WORD/RELYING ON YOURSELF

In Isaiah 7, the instruction the Lord has given to those going through challenges is found in verse 4. We need to focus on what the Lord is saying rather than on the challenges. We need to focus on what the Word says and do just that. **Proverbs 3:5-6** says:

> *"Trust in the Lord with all your heart; do not depend on your own understanding. Seek His will in ALL you do, and He will direct your paths."* [NLT]

7. WORRYING

Philippians 4:6-9 NLT says,

> *"don't worry about anything; instead, pray about everything. Tell God what you need and thank Him for all He has done. If you do this, you*

will experience God's peace, which is far more wonderful than the human mind can understand. His peace will guard your hearts and minds as you live in Christ Jesus. And now, dear brothers and sisters, let me say one more thing as I close this letter. Fix your thoughts on what is true and honourable and right. Think about things that are pure and lovely and admirable. Think about things that are excellent and worthy of praise. Keep putting into practice all you learned from me and heard from me and saw me doing, and the God of peace will be with you.

8. HANGING OUT WITH THE WRONG CROWD

The Bible says in **Proverbs 12:26,**

The righteous shall choose his friends wisely.

1 Corinthians 15:33 says,

"Do not be deceived, evil communication corrupts good manners."

Proverbs 13:20 says,

"He who moves with the wise shall become wise, but the companion of fools shall be destroyed."

It does matter the crowd or person you choose to hang out with. Fear and doubt and worry are all contagious and will definitely affect your faith.

Deuteronomy 20:1-4 makes it quite clear that God goes with us to fight for us and as such we are not to be afraid but rather put our trust (faith) in God Almighty. In verse 8 it says,

"The officers shall speak further to the people, and say, "What man is there who is fearful and fainthearted? Let him go and return to his house, lest the heart of his brethren faint like his heart."

This clearly shows that fear is contagious. You shouldn't move with those who tell you that you can't make it.

Elisha said in **2 Kings 3:14,**

"As the Lord of hosts lives, before whom I stand, surely were it not that I regard the presence of Jehoshaphat king of Judah, I would not look at you, nor see you."

To show how important faith is in this journey of life, the Book of Hebrews Chapter Eleven is known as the Hall of Faith because it gives a list of men and women in the Bible who despite all the odds were able to overcome impossible situations and circumstances by exercising FAITH. Now it makes even more sense why **1 John 5:4** says that what overcomes the world for us is our FAITH. Without FAITH it is impossible to please God Almighty.

THE HALL OF FAITH: HEBREWS CHAPTER 11 [AMP]

Even as there is what is known as the Hall of Fame in the world, there is also the Hall of Faith in the Bible, and some believers of today can be said to have made that list seeing how they have conducted themselves even in the face of trials and challenges.

The Book of Hebrews Chapter 11 can be called the Hall of Fame in the Bible, and by studying that Chapter, it is my utmost hope that we can know that despite the situation we may be in at any time, victory is assured once we put our faith to work.

Now FAITH is the assurance (the confirmation, the title deed) of the things [we] hope for, being the proof [we] do not see and the conviction of their reality [FAITH perceiving as real fact what is not revealed to the senses]. For by [FAITH-trust and holy fervour born of FAITH] the men of old had divine testimony borne to them and obtained a good report. By FAITH we understand that the worlds [during the successive ages] were framed (fashioned, put in order, and equipped for their intended purpose) by the word of God, so that what we see was not made out of things which are visible. Prompted, actuated] by FAITH Abel brought God a better and more acceptable sacrifice than Cain, because of which it was testified of him that he was righteous [that he was upright and in right standing with God], and God bore witness by accepting and acknowledging his gifts. And though he died, yet [through the incident] he is still speaking.

Because of FAITH, Enoch was caught up and transferred to heaven, so that he did not have a glimpse of death; and he was not found, because God had translated him. For even before he was taken to heaven, he received testimony [still on record] that he had pleased and satisfactory with God. But without FAITH it is impossible to please and be satisfactory to Him. For whoever would come near to God must [necessarily] believe that God exists and that He is the rewarder of those who earnestly and diligently seek Him [out].

Prompted by FAITH, Noah, being forewarned by God concerning events of which as yet there was no visible sign, took heed and diligently and reverently constructed and prepared an ark for the deliverance of his own family. By this [his FAITH which relied on God] he passed judgement and sentence on the world's unbelief and became an heir and possessor of righteousness (that relation of being right into which God puts the person who has FAITH).

(Urged on) by FAITH, Abraham, when he was called, obeyed and went forth to a place which he was destined to receive as an inheritance; and

he went, although he did not know or trouble his mind about where he was to go. By FAITH he sojourned in the land of promise, as in a strange country, dwelling in tabernacles with Isaac and Jacob, the heirs with him of the same promise. For he was [waiting expectantly and confidently] looking forward to the city which has fixed and firm foundations, whose Architect and Builder is God. Because of FAITH also Sarah herself received physical power to conceive a child, even when she was long past the age for it, because she considered [God] who had given her the promise to be reliable and trustworthy and true to His word.

So from one man, though he was physically as good as dead, there have sprung descendants whose number is as the stars of heaven and as countless as the innumerable sands on the seashore. These people all died controlled and sustained by their FAITH, but not having received the tangible fulfilment of [God's] promises, only having seen it and greeted it from a great distance by FAITH, and all the while acknowledging and confessing that they were strangers and temporary residents and exiles upon the earth. Now those people who talk as they did show plainly that they are in search of a fatherland of their own country). If they had been thinking with [homesick] remembrance of that country from which they were immigrants, they would have found constant opportunity to return to it. But the truth is that they were yearning for and aspiring to a better and more desirable country, that is, a heavenly [one].

For that reason, God is not ashamed to be called their God {even to be surnamed their God-the God of Abraham, Isaac, and Jacob}, for He has prepared a city for them. By faith Abraham, when he was put to the test [while the testing of his FAITH was still in progress], had already brought Isaac for an offering; he who had gladly received and welcomed [God's] promises was ready to sacrifice his only son. Of whom it was said, Through Isaac shall your descendants be reckoned. For he reasoned that God was able to raise [him] up even from among the dead. Indeed, in the sense that Isaac was figuratively dead [potentially sacrificed], he did [actually] receive him back from the dead. {With eyes of} FAITH Isaac, looking far into the future, invoked blessings upon Jacob and Esau.

[Prompted] by FAITH, Jacob, when he was dying, blessed each of Joseph's sons and bowed in prayer over the top of his staff. [Actuated] by FAITH Joseph, when nearing the end of his life, referred to [the promise of God for] the departure of the Israelites out of Egypt and gave instructions concerning the burial of his own bones.

[Prompted] by FAITH, Moses after his birth, was kept concealed for three months by his parents, because they saw how comely the child was; and they were not overawed and terrified by the king's decree. [Aroused] by FAITH Moses, when he had grown to maturity and become great, refused to be called the son of Pharaoh's daughter, because he preferred to share the oppression [suffer the hardships] and bear the shame of the people of God rather than to have the fleeting enjoyment of a sinful life. He considered the contempt and abuse and shame [borne for] the Christ (the Messiah who was to come) to be greater wealth than all the treasures of Egypt, for he looked forward and away to reward (recompense). [Motivated] by FAITH he left Egypt behind him, being unawed and undismayed by the wrath of the king; for he never flinched but held staunchly to his purpose and endured steadfastly as one who gazed on Him who is invisible.

By FAITH (simple trust and confidence in God) he instituted and carried out Passover and the sprinkling of the blood [on the doorposts], so that the destroyer of the firstborn (the angel) might not touch those [of the children of Israel]. [Urged on] by FAITH the people crossed the Red Sea as [though] on dry land, but when the Egyptians tried to do the same thing, they were swallowed up [by the sea]. Because of FAITH the walls of Jericho fell down after they had been encompassed for seven days [by the Israelites].

[Prompted] by FAITH Rahab the prostitute was not destroyed along with those who refused to believe and obey, because she had received the spies in peace [without enmity]. And what shall I say further? For time will fail me to tell of Gideon, Barak, Samson, Jephthah, of David and Samuel and the Prophets, who by [the help of] FAITH subdued kingdoms, administered justice, obtained promised blessings, closed the mouth of lions. Extinguished the power of raging fire, escaped the devouring of the sword, out of frailty and weakness won strength and became stalwart, even mighty and resistless in battle, routing alien hosts.

[Some] women received again their dead by a resurrection. Others were tortured to death with clubs, refusing to accept release [offered on the terms of denying their FAITH], so that they might be resurrected to a better life. Others had to suffer the trial of mocking and scourging and even chains and imprisonment. They were stoned to death; they were lured with tempting offers [to renounce their FAITH]; they were sawn asunder; they were slaughtered by the sword; [while they were alive] they had to go about wrapped in the skins of sheep and goats, utterly destitute, oppressed, cruelly treated. [Men] of whom the world was not worthy- roaming over the desolate places and the mountains, and [living] in caves and caverns and holes of the earth. And all of these, though they won divine approval by [means of] their FAITH, did not receive the fulfilment of what was promised. Because God had us in mind and had something better and greater in view for us, so that they [these heroes and heroines of FAITH] should not come to perfection apart from us [before we could join them].

This is the Hall of FAITH. Will you join them by putting your faith to work? God is no respecter of persons. May we all see our names engraved in diamond on the plaque of the Hall of Faith. Amen.

PRAYER OF SALVATION

Heavenly Father, I come before You today by the shed blood of Your Son, Jesus Christ, and I have assurance that You will not cast me away. Dear Lord Jesus, I confess to You that I am a sinner, and I ask that You forgive my sins and cleanse me with Your Precious Blood.
Write my name in the Book of Life. Restore unto me the lost years of my life. Infill me with Your own Spirit and grant me the grace to be Your witness from now onwards until You come to take me home to spend eternity with You, Amen.

ABOUT THE BOOK

*"God did not raise that Pastor from the dead because I prayed, since I was not even aware that a dead body was brought to the crusade venue. He was raised from the dead because of his wife's **'Stubborn Faith.'"***
— Reinhard Bonnie

Do you believe in God, but struggle to live your faith in the face of daily challenges? In *Stubborn Faith*, Pastor Lawrence Oji shares his transformative journey from skepticism to unshakeable belief. Fueled by a powerful encounter with God in Pakistan, he unveils a practical guide to cultivating deep, unwavering trust in the midst of life's uncertainties. The book delves into the rawness of living by faith—a path that's not always easy, but infinitely rewarding. In the book, you will discover:

- Why "blind trust" is the key to unlocking God's promises.
- How to navigate life's storms with unwavering confidence, even when the path ahead seems unclear.
- A powerful testament to the transformative power of faith—beginning with the author's own transformation from drug addiction and despair to a life of hope and purpose.

Stubborn Faith is more than just a book; it's an invitation to step outside of doubt, to embrace the radical belief that faith is the only currency you need, and to witness the transformative power of God's unwavering love in your life. Are you ready to unleash the power of "Stubborn Faith" in your own life?

OTHER BOOKS BY THE AUTHOR

- *From Prison To Pulpit: One man's true story of God's life changing power*
- *Soul Winning Made Simple: Step By Step Guide to Personal Evangelism*
- *Not Without A Scar: Choices and Consequences*
- *Positioned By Grace*
- *Depression: The Silent Killer*

For Prayer and Counselling you can contact me freely on

Mobile: 07889080268

Email: solutionministries2001@yahoo.com

Pastor Lawrence Solution Oji

ABOUT THE AUTHOR

Pastor Lawrence Oji (MA Theology, University of Roehampton) also known as 'Pastor Solution' is a testament to God's amazing grace. Despite a turbulent past marked by multiple career changes, and addiction, Pastor Oji ultimately embraced redemption, transforming from a star student gone astray (while undergoing his university education in Chandigarh, India) to a passionate evangelist. His journey from being the youngest Inspector of Police in Nigeria to a life of drugs and imprisonment ultimately led him to a transformative encounter with God's grace in prison. Now, he has dedicated his life to sharing this transformative grace with others, particularly prisoners, prostitutes, and drug addicts around the world, leaving behind a trail of changed lives through his preaching and notable books like *From Prison To Pulpit, Soul Winning Made Simple*, and *Not Without A Scar*. He is married to Ugozamba (Mrs. Stella Angel Oji), and they are blessed with three children.

Printed in Great Britain
by Amazon

37337399R00106